KU-416-583

NUTCASES

CONTRACT LAW

AUSTRALIA
Law Book Co.
Sydney

CANADA and USA
Carswell
Toronto

HONG KONG
Sweet & Maxwell Asia

NEW ZEALAND
Brookers
Wellington

SINGAPORE and MALAYSIA
Sweet & Maxwell Asia
Singapore and Kuala Lumpur

NUTCASES

CONTRACT LAW

THIRD EDITION

by

ANNE RUFF, LL.B., LL.M.
Barrister
Principal Lecturer in Law, Middlesex University

London • Sweet & Maxwell • 2002

First edition 1996
Reprinted 1998, 1999, 2000
Second edition 1999
Reprinted 2001
Third edition 2002
Reprinted 2003
Reprinted 2004

Published in 2002 by
Sweet & Maxwell Limited of
100 Avenue Road, London, NW3 3PF
http://www.sweetandmaxwell.co.uk

Typeset by LBJ Typesetting Ltd of Kingsclere
Printed in Great Britain by Creative Print and Design
(Wales) Ebbw Vale

No natural forests were destroyed to make this product:
only farmed timber was used and replanted

ISBN 0–421–76750 2

**A CIP Catalogue record for this book is available
from the British Library**

All rights reserved. Crown copyright is
reproduced with the permission of the Controller of HMSO
and the Queen's Printer for Scotland.

No part of this publication may be reproduced or
transmitted in any form or by any means,
or stored in any retrieval system of any
nature without prior written
permission, except for permitted
fair dealing under the
Copyright, Designs and Patents Act 1988, or in
accordance with the terms of a licence issued by the
Licensing Agency in respect of photocopying and/or
reprographic reproduction.
Application for permission for other use of copyright
material including permission to reproduce extracts in
other published works shall be made to the publishers.
Full acknowledgment of author, publisher and source
must be given.

©
Sweet & Maxwell
2002

CONTENTS

TABLE OF CASES

(Bold type indicates where cases are dealt with in more detail.)

TABLE OF STATUTES

1. INTRODUCTION

The Key Characteristics of a Contract

Agreement—Promise—Voluntary

Key Principle: **Contractual obligations are based on agreement. The existence of an agreement is objectively determined.**

G. Percy Trentham Ltd v. Archital Luxfer Ltd 1993
The plaintiffs T obtained quotations from the defendants A for the design, supply and installation of windows. The parties continued to negotiate both orally and in writing over the contract terms. The defendants undertook the required work and the plaintiffs paid them for it. There were defects in the windows and the plaintiffs claimed that the defendants were in breach of contract. The defendants denied that any contract had come into existence.

Held: (CA) Where the transaction was fully performed a contract could be concluded by conduct, or come into existence during performance. There was therefore a legally binding contract. The parties plainly intended to enter into such a contract. [1993] 1 Lloyd's Rep. 25

Commentary
Steyn L.J. stated that English law generally adopts an objective rather than a subjective theory of contract formation. The governing criterion is the reasonable expectations of honest men. (See also Chapter 2, p. 6, and *BSC v. Cleveland Bridge and Engineering Co. Ltd* (1984) (see p. 4)).

Key Principle: **A promise is usually the basis of a contractual obligation. It is normally a statement as to future conduct rather than a statement of present fact.**

Kleinwort Benson Ltd v. Malaysia Mining Corporation Berhad 1989
The defendants formed a subsidiary company M. The plaintiff bankers lent a total of £10 million to the subsidiary company

having relied on a "comfort letter" provided by the defendants to the plaintiffs. In the letter the defendants stated that: "It is our policy to ensure that the business of [M] is at all times in a position to meet its liabilities to you." M ceased trading and did not pay its debts. The plaintiffs asked the defendants to ensure that they were repaid the money owed to them by M. The defendants refused to do so and claimed that the defendant's statement did not impose a legally binding obligation upon them to pay off their subsidiary's debts.

Held: (CA) The statement in the comfort letter was not a contractually binding promise. It was a statement of present fact not a statement that the policy would be continued in the future. Therefore the plaintiffs were unable to recover any of the money lent to M. [1989] 1 W.L.R. 379

Commentary
(1) The Court of Appeal commented that the consequences of the decision by the defendants to repudiate their moral responsibility to ensure that the plaintiffs were repaid, were not matters that the court should consider.
(2) A comfort letter is a letter written usually by a parent company, but it could be by a government, to the lender of money, giving comfort to the lender about a loan made to a subsidiary company or a public entity. It is commonly used where the "guarantor" is not willing to accept a legally binding commitment.
(3) Whether a letter of comfort is intended to be legally binding is a question of fact.

Key Principle: **Contracts are agreements which are voluntarily entered into by both parties.**

Norweb plc v. Dixon 1995
The appellants N were under a statutory duty to supply electricity upon being required to do so by the owner or occupier of any premises. The respondent D made such a request. One of the issues that arose was whether such an arrangement amounted to a contract.

Held: (QBD) The legal compulsion as to both the creation of the relationship between a public electricity supplier and a tariff customer, and the fixing of its terms, is inconsistent with the existence of a contract. The supply of electricity in these circumstances is governed by statute not by contract. [1995] 1 W.L.R 636

Commentary

Compare *Balfour Beatty Construction (Scotland) v. Scottish Power* (1994) (see p. 169). See also *AE Beckett & Sons (Lyndons) Ltd v. Midland Electricity plc* [2001] 1 W.L.R. 281 where a claim in negligence for economic loss was successfully brought against an electricity supplier by a customer.

Contract—Tort—Restitution

Key Principle: **The same set of facts may give rise to liability in the tort of negligence as well as in contract.**

Muirhead v. Industrial Tank Specialities Ltd and others 1986

The plaintiff was a wholesale fish merchant. The first defendants I.T.S. entered into a contract with the plaintiff for the supply and installation of a tank and pumps for the storage of live lobsters. The manufacturers of the pumps, Leroy Somer Electric Motors Ltd, were the third defendants. The pumps were defective and the whole stock of lobsters died. The plaintiff claimed compensation for the lobsters, the loss of profit on the intended sales, and other consequential financial losses. The plaintiff was successful in his claim against I.T.S., but the company went into liquidation and no money was forthcoming. The plaintiff continued with his claim against the third defendants. Since there was no contract between the plaintiff and the third defendants this claim was brought in the tort of negligence.

Held: (CA) The plaintiff could recover damages in tort from the third defendants because it was reasonably foreseeable that if the pumps failed to work then the lobsters would suffer physical harm. The plaintiff could also recover any financial loss caused by the death of the lobsters. [1986] Q.B. 507

Commentary

However, the Court of Appeal further stated that the plaintiff could not recover damages for pure economic loss from the third defendants. The loss of profit on the intended sales appears to have been regarded as pure economic loss. The court considered that such loss was only recoverable from I.T.S., the other party to the contract. However, loss of intended future profits is not always recoverable in a contract claim (see *Parsons v. Uttley Ingham* (1978) (see p. 168)).

Key Principle: **If the parties to a contract intend their relationship to be governed solely by the contract then a court will not impose a concurrent liability in tort.**

Greater Nottingham Co-Operative Society Ltd v. Cementation Piling and Foundations Ltd 1989

The plaintiffs were owners of a building. They entered into a building contract with the main contractor. The defendant sub-contractors also entered into a contract with the main contractor. In addition the plaintiffs entered into a collateral contract with the defendants, but the contract did not impose liability on the defendants for negligent performance of the contract. The defendants negligently operated drilling equipment which caused physical damage and financial loss. The plaintiffs sued the defendants in the tort of negligence.

Held: (CA) The plaintiffs could not recover for the financial loss. Entering into a collateral contract was inconsistent with the existence of liability in the tort of negligence. [1989] Q.B. 71

Commentary

Note that concurrent liability in contract and tort may arise, e.g. liability for careless statements and liability of solicitors to their clients. The duty of care in tort may be wider in scope than the contractual obligation (*Holt v. Payne Skillington (a Firm) C.A., The Times*, December 22, 1995, CA).

Key Principle: **Restitution may provide a remedy to a party who has rendered performance or paid money where in fact there is no valid contract.**

British Steel Corporation v. Cleveland Bridge and Engineering Co Ltd 1984

The plaintiffs were asked by the defendants to produce cast-steel nodes. The plaintiffs produced an initial estimate, but discussions continued about the precise specifications of the nodes. The defendants then sent a "letter of intent" to the plaintiffs which, *inter alia*, asked them to start work immediately, which they did. Negotiations continued about the specifications, the payment and liability for loss for late delivery. All the nodes were delivered apart from one which was delayed because of an industrial dispute at the plaintiff's plant. The plaintiffs claimed a reasonable price (*quantum meruit*) for the nodes, arguing that no agreement had been reached by the parties. The defendants refused to pay for the nodes and counterclaimed for damages for breach of contract because of, inter alia, the late delivery of one node.

Held: (QBD) Since the parties had not reached agreement on the price and other essential terms, such as liability for late delivery, no contract had been entered into by them for the manufacture of the nodes. However, the defendants were bound to pay a reasonable sum for the manufacture of the nodes as it was done at their request. [1984] 1 All E.R. 504

Commentary
(1) A *quantum meruit* claim is an example of a action based on the equitable principle of restitution. Such a claim is sometimes classified as "quasi-contract". In *Lipkin Gorman v. Karpnale Ltd* [1991] 2 A.C. 548 the House of Lords recognised for the first time the existence of a principle of restitution based upon unjust enrichment. Restitution like tort and contract comes under the umbrella of the law of obligations.
(2) Such a claim, as opposed to a claim for breach of contract, is unlikely to enable recovery of any future losses.

Key Principle: **Costs incurred by way of accelerated performance of an anticipated contract which does not materialise are recoverable under the law of restitution.**

Regalian Properties Plc v. London Docklands Development Corporation 1995
In 1986 the plaintiffs and defendants began negotiations for the development of land for housing in Wapping. The plaintiffs offered £18.5 million for a licence to build, which the defendants accepted "subject to contract". Various delays meant that the

building work did not start, and in 1988 the market value of residential land fell so much that it was not worth proceeding. The plaintiffs claimed £3 million from the defendants as reimbursement for the costs they incurred in preparing for the proposed contract.

Held: (ChD) The plaintiffs were unsuccessful because they incurred the costs for the purpose of putting themselves in a position to obtain and then perform the contract, rather than by way of accelerated performance. [1995] 1 W.L.R. 212

Commentary
BSC v. Cleveland Bridge and Engineering Co. Ltd (1984) (see p. 4) was distinguished.

2. THE AGREEMENT

The Formation of an Agreement

Introduction

Key Principle: **Offer and acceptance will, in the vast majority of cases, represent the mechanism of contract formation.**

G Percy Trentham Ltd v. Archital Luxfer Ltd 1993
The facts and the decision are set out at p. 1.

Held: (CA) Steyn L.J. considered, *obiter*, that there are four matters of importance in contract formation.

(1) English law generally adopts an objective theory of contract formation.

(2) The coincidence of offer and acceptance will in the vast majority of cases represent the mechanism of contract formation.

(3) Where a transaction has been performed by both parties the court is more likely to find that there is a binding contract.

(4) Where a contract only comes into existence during and as a result of performance the court is likely to hold that the contract impliedly and retrospectively covers pre-contractual performance.

Offer

Key Principle: **An offer is a statement which objectively indicates that the offeror is prepared to contract on specified terms.**

Gibson v. Manchester City Council 1979

The plaintiff wanted to buy his council house from the defendant Council. The Council wrote to him stating that it "may be prepared to sell the house" to him and inviting him to make a "formal application to buy" on the enclosed application form. He did so using the Council's printed form which stated "I . . . now wish to purchase my council house." Four months later the Council informed the plaintiff that it was not prepared to sell him the house. The plaintiff claimed that the Council's first letter was an offer which he had accepted when he submitted the application form, and so there was a binding contract.

Held: (HL) There was no binding contract. The words used made it quite impossible to construe the Council's letter to the plaintiff as a contractual offer capable of being converted into a legally enforceable contract by the plaintiff's written acceptance. The letter was just a step in the negotiations. [1979] 1 W.L.R. 294

Commentary

(1) Lord Diplock favoured the conventional approach of looking to see whether, on the true construction of the documents, there is an offer and an acceptance. He disagreed with Lord Denning's view in the Court of Appeal that the court should look at the correspondence as a whole and the conduct of the parties to see whether they have reached agreement.

(2) Compare *Storer v. Manchester City Council* [1974] 1 W.L.R. 1403 where the Court of Appeal held that the council house tenant had accepted the Council's offer to sell when he signed and returned an Agreement for Sale to the Council.

Key Principle: **An offer can be made to the world at large and it can be accepted by anybody who performs the necessary actions.**

Carlill v. Carbolic Smoke Ball Co. 1893

In a newspaper advertisement the Carbolic Smoke Ball Co. stated that it would pay £100 to any person who became ill with flu after using the smoke ball as directed and that to show its sincerity it had deposited £1,000 in a bank account. Mrs Carlill used the smoke ball, but nevertheless caught flu.

Held: (CA) The advertisement was an offer to the world which was accepted by Mrs Carlill when she used the smoke ball as directed. She was entitled to the £100. [1893] 1 Q.B. 256

Commentary
(1) Newspaper advertisements are usually considered to be invitations to treat. See, *e.g. Partridge v. Crittenden* (1968) (see p. 9).
(2) This is an example of a unilateral offer and acceptance (see p. 15). If such an offer is revoked, the revocation does not have to be communicated to every single offeree.
(3) The consideration for the Company's promise to pay was the inconvenience suffered by Mrs Carlill when using the smoke ball and the likely increase in sales for the Company.

———

Key Principle: **A notice displayed prominently in a tour operator's office was an offer to the world.**

Bowerman v. Association of British Travel Agents Ltd 1995
P booked a school skiing holiday with a tour operator who was a member of ABTA. The holiday was later cancelled when the tour operator ceased to trade. ABTA refunded all payments made, except for insurance premiums of £10.00 which the plaintiffs sued to recover. The appeal turned on the construction of a notice which each ABTA tour operator was required to display prominently in its office.

Held: (CA) The notice setting out ABTA's scheme of financial protection for holiday makers was promissory in nature and intended to be legally binding. (*The Times*, November 24, 1995).

Commentary
The notice was an offer which the customer accepted by choosing to book a holiday with an ABTA member (Carlill v. Carbolic Smoke Ball Co (1893) applied).

Key Principle: **An offer must contain an express or implied promise.**

Harvey v. Facey 1893
The appellant sent a telegram to the respondent asking "Will you sell us Bumper Hall Pen? Telegraph lowest cash price." The respondent replied, "Lowest cash price for Bumper Hall Pen £900." The appellant agreed to buy the property for £900.

Held: (JCPC) The respondent's reply was not an offer containing a promise, it was merely a response to the second question in the appellant's telegram. [1893] A.C. 552

Invitations to Treat Distinguished From Offers

Key Principle: **Advertisements are normally invitations to treat because it is clear that the advertiser does not intend to be bound.**

Partridge v. Crittenden 1968
The defendant placed an advertisement in a magazine stating "Bramblefinch cocks and hens, 25s".

Held: (DC) The advertisement did not amount to an offer to sell. [1968] 1 W.L.R. 1204

Key Principle: **An advertisement for an auction is normally an invitation to treat, and the bid is the offer which can be accepted by the auctioneer.**

Harris v. Nickerson 1873
The defendant auctioneer advertised that certain items including "office furniture" were to be sold at an auction sale. The plaintiff attended the sale to buy the office furniture, but it was withdrawn from the sale. The plaintiff claimed that the advertisement amounted to an offer to sell the furniture which he accepted by attending the auction.

Held: (Q.B.) The advertisement did not amount to a promise to sell the furniture. (1873) L.R. 8 Q.B. 286

Key Principle: **At an auction without reserve, the auctioneer is bound to sell to the highest bidder.**

Barry v. Davies (t/a Heathcote Ball & Co) 2000
The auctioneer withdrew two engine analysers from an auction without reserve because he considered that the bids were too low.

Held: (CA) There was a collateral agreement that the auctioneer would sell to the highest bidder. The auctioneer was liable to pay damages to the highest bidder, amounting to the difference between the highest bid (£400) and the market price of the machines (£28,000). [2001] 1 All E.R. 944

Commentary
Note that in this case, unlike *Harris v. Nickerson* (above), the auctioneer only withdrew the goods after the bidding had started.

Key Principle: **A circular inviting the submission of tenders is normally an invitation to treat and the submission of the tender is the offer.**

Spencer v. Harding 1870
The defendant sent out a circular inviting tenders for the purchase of stock. The plaintiffs submitted the highest tender, but the defendant refused to sell the stock to them.

Held: The circular was not an offer to sell to the highest bidder, it was merely inviting offers to buy. (1870) L.R. 5 C.P. 561

Commentary
Note that different principles apply to the acceptance of tenders which are standing offers. See *Great Northern Railway v. Witham* (1873) (see p. 16).

Key Principle: **An invitation to submit tenders is an offer to open and consider all conforming tenders together.**

Blackpool and Fylde Aero Club Ltd v. Blackpool Borough Council 1990

The defendant local authority invited tenders for a concession to operate pleasure flights from the local airport. The letter stated that "No tender which is received after the last date and time specified" would be considered. The plaintiff's tender was posted by hand in the defendant's letter box before the deadline expired, but the defendant's staff did not empty the box and the plaintiff's tender was not considered.

Held: (CA) It was implied that all tenders submitted which complied with the tendering procedure would be opened and considered together with other conforming tenders. The invitation to tender was a unilateral offer which was accepted by the submission of a tender. [1990] 1 W.L.R. 1195

Commentary
English and E.C. legislation regulates invitations to tender issued by local authorities for public works and public service contracts.

Key Principle: **An invitation to submit tenders may amount to an offer where it is clear that the seller intends to sell to the highest bidder.**

Harvela Investments Ltd v. Royal Trust Co. of Canada 1985

The defendant invited the plaintiff and a third party to make an offer for the purchase of shares and undertook to accept the highest offer. The plaintiff offered $2,175,000, while the third party offered $2,100,000 or $101,000 in excess of any other offer. The defendant accepted the third party's bid because they thought they were obliged to do so. The plaintiff sought an injunction.

Held: (HL) The third party's bid was a referential bid and was not a valid offer. The defendant's invitation was an offer which was accepted by the submission of the highest valid bid. [1985] 3 W.L.R. 276

Key Principle: **The display of goods for sale on a super-market shelf is an invitation to treat, and the offer to buy is made by the customer presenting the goods to the cashier.**

Pharmaceutical Society of Great Britain v. Boots Cash Chemists Ltd 1953

The defendants, Boots, displayed medicines on their shelves which under statute must be sold under the supervision of a registered pharmacist. In this shop the pharmacist could refuse to allow the purchase at the cash desk.

Held: (CA) The contract of sale occurred at the cash desk not when the customer took the medicines off the shelves and placed them in a basket, and so the statutory requirement was satisfied. [1953] 2 W.L.R. 427

Commentary

(1) This principle also applies to a display of goods in a shop window: *Fisher v. Bell* [1961] 1 Q.B. 394 display of flick knives. Note that a number of the above cases have arisen because it is a criminal offence to "offer for sale" a particular item.

(2) It is not clear whether the offer is accepted when the seller asks for the price or when the buyer pays the money.

Termination of Offer

Key Principle: **If no time is fixed for an offer to lapse, then it lapses after the passage of a reasonable time.**

Ramsgate Victoria Hotel Co. Ltd v. Montefiore 1866

In June the defendant offered to buy shares in the plaintiff's company and paid a deposit. The plaintiffs informed him at the end of November that he had been allocated shares and that the balance was now due.

Held: The defendant was entitled to refuse to take up the shares. His offer had lapsed because an excessive amount of time had passed. (1866) L.R. 1 Ex. 109

Commentary

What is reasonable is a question of fact and will depend upon the subject-matter and the context of the contract.

Key Principle: **An offer can be revoked by the offeror at any time before acceptance, but the revocation is only effective once it is communicated to the offeree.**

Byrne v. Van Tienhoven 1880
On October 1, the defendants posted a letter in Cardiff to the plaintiffs in New York offering to sell them tin plates. On October 8, the defendants revoked their offer by post. On October 11, the plaintiffs accepted the offer by telegraph, and confirmed their acceptance by a letter dated October 15. On October 20, the plaintiffs received the defendants' letter of revocation.

Held: The revocation of the offer was not effective because it was only communicated on October 20, which was after the acceptance of the offer on October 11. (1880) 5 C.P.D. 344

Commentary
The communication can be made through a third party: *Dickinson v. Dodds* [1876] 2 Ch.D. 463. Treitel has criticised this decision because it leads to uncertainty.

Key Principle: **Actual communication of the revocation to a particular individual is not necessary where the offer has been made to a company.**

The Brimnes 1975
The defendants hired a ship from the plaintiffs, but did not pay the hire due by a particular date, so the plaintiffs sent a telex message withdrawing the use of the ship from the defendants.

Held: (CA) The withdrawal was effective when the telex arrived at the defendants' office during ordinary business hours. [1975] Q.B. 929

Commentary
(1) Although this case concerned the termination of a contract rather than the withdrawal of an offer, it is likely that the principle as to communication is the same.

(2) Nor is actual communication of the revocation necessary where a unilateral offer (see *Carlill v. Carbolic Smoke Ball Co.* (1893)) is revoked. The offeror is required to take reasonable steps to bring notice of the revocation to anyone who was likely to be aware of the original offer.

Key Principle: **An attempt to accept an offer on new terms, not contained in the offer, is a rejection of the offer accompanied by a counter-offer.**

Hyde v. Wrench 1840
The defendant offered to sell his farm to the plaintiff for £1,000. The plaintiff responded by offering to buy it for £950. The defendant refused to sell it for that amount. The plaintiff then tried to accept the defendant's original offer to sell for £1,000.

Held: There was no contract. Having rejected the defendant's offer to sell by his offer of £950, the plaintiff could not then revive and accept the defendant's offer. (1840) 49 All E.R. Rep. 132

Commentary
In *Society of Lloyd's v. Twinn, The Times*, April 4, 2000, the Vice-Chancellor stated that there was no reason why an offeree should not accept an offer unconditionally and, at the same time, make a collateral offer to the original offer. Whether a particular statement amounts to a counter offer or a collateral offer is a question of fact.

Key Principle: **A request for information in response to an offer is not a rejection and counter-offer.**

Stevenson, Jacques & Co. v. McLean 1880
The plaintiffs and the defendants were negotiating about the sale of iron. The defendant wrote offering to sell the iron for cash. The plaintiff telegraphed asking whether the iron could be delivered over a two-month period.

Held: The plaintiff's telegraph was not a rejection of the defendant's offer it was merely an inquiry, and so the plaintiff could subsequently accept the defendant's offer. (1880) 5 QBD 346.

Acceptance

Key Principle: **An acceptance must amount to a final and unqualified assent to the terms of the offer.**

Butler Machine Tool Co. v. Ex-Cell-o Corporation Ltd 1979
The plaintiffs offered to sell a machine tool to the defendants for £75,535, delivery to be in 10 months' time. The plaintiffs' offer included a price variation clause, and stated that their terms and conditions would prevail over any terms and conditions in the defendants' order. The defendants placed an order on their own terms and conditions, which did not include a price variation clause. At the bottom of the defendants' order was a tear-off acknowledgment slip for completion by the plaintiffs, which stated: "We accept your order on the terms and conditions stated thereon". The plaintiffs completed, signed and returned the slip with a letter stating that the order had been entered in accordance with their original offer. The plaintiffs delivered the machine and relied on their price variation clause to increase the price by £2,892. The defendants refused to pay.

Held: (CA) The defendants' terms prevailed and so the price variation clause was not a term of the contract. The defendants' order was not an acceptance because it contained additional requirements. It was a rejection and counter-offer, which was accepted when the plaintiffs returned the acknowledgment slip. [1979] 1 W.L.R. 401

Commentary
(1) This is an example of "battle of the forms" where both parties use standard forms in their business, which they do not appear to have read!
(2) See also *Hyde v. Wrench* (1840) (see p. 14).

Key Principle: **Acceptance can be by words or by conduct.**

Brogden v. Metropolitan Railway Co. 1877
After supplying coal to the railway company for some years, Brogden agreed to a draft contract proposed by the company.

The company inadvertently never formally accepted the contract. Nevertheless the company ordered and Brogden supplied coal in accordance with its terms. A dispute arose and Brogden claimed that no binding contract existed.

Held: (HL) There was a binding agreement because both parties acted upon the draft and treated it as binding. The company ordered the coal and Brogden supplied it, which showed that the offer was accepted. [1877] 2 App. Cas. 666

Commentary
See also *G. Percy Trentham Ltd v. Archital Luxfer Ltd* (1993) (see p. 1).

Key Principle: **Acceptance of a standing offer occurs when an order is placed.**

Great Northern Railway v. Witham 1873
The plaintiff advertised for tenders for the supply of railway stores. The defendant submitted a tender offering to provide the required articles for 12 months. The plaintiff placed orders, all of which were carried out except for the last one. The defendant argued that he was not legally obliged to supply the goods, and so was not in breach of contract.

Held: The agreement to supply for a year was a standing offer which was accepted each time an order was placed. [1873] L.R. 9 C.P. 16

Commentary
(1) A standing offer arises where the offeror agrees to supply goods or services as and when required over a specific period.
(2) A standing offer can be revoked at any time before acceptance.
(3) Placing the order is also consideration for the offeror's promise to supply goods over a period of time.

Key Principle: **Where there is a unilateral offer acceptance occurs when the offeree fully performs the required act.**

Carlill v. Carbolic Smoke Ball Co. 1893
(see p. 7)

Held: (CA) The advertisement was an offer to the world which was accepted by Mrs Carlill when she used the smoke ball as directed. She was entitled to the £100. [1893] 1 Q.B. 256

Commentary
(1) There is no need for the offeree to give advance notice of acceptance to the offeror.
(2) It has not been settled when acceptance of a unilateral offer takes place. Is it when the offeree starts to perform the condition or when performance is complete? In *Daulia Ltd v. Four Millbank Nominees Ltd* [1978] 2 All E.R. 557 the Court of Appeal considered that a unilateral offer could not be withdrawn once performance had started.

Communication of Acceptance

Key Principle: **Acceptance of an offer must be communicated to the offeror.**

Holwell Securities Ltd v. Hughes 1974
The plaintiff had an option to purchase property from the defendant. Clause 2 of the option agreement stated: "The said option shall be exercisable by notice in writing to the Defendant at any time within 6 months from the date hereof". The plaintiff's solicitors wrote a letter to the defendant giving notice of the exercise of the option. The letter was posted, properly addressed and stamped but was never actually delivered to the defendant. Was there an effective communication of the plaintiff's acceptance? [1974] 1 W.L.R. 155

Held: (CA) The words "notice . . . to" in the option agreement required actual communication of the acceptance, and so no contract came into force.

Commentary
The plaintiff unsuccessfully argued that the postal rule (see pp. 18–19) applied and that there was a valid contract.

Key Principle: **An acceptance by telex has no effect until it is received by the offeror.**

Entores v. Miles Far East Corporation 1955
The plaintiffs in London made an offer to the defendants in Amsterdam. The defendants accepted by telex. Was the contract entered into in Amsterdam where the telex was sent or in London where it was received?

Held: (CA) The contract was only complete when the acceptance was received by the plaintiffs in London. [1955] 3 W.L.R. 48

Commentary
This principle is applicable to other forms of instantaneous communications such as telephone, and presumably also to fax and email.

Key Principle: **No universal rule can cover the many variations in telex communications.**

Brinkibon Ltd v. Stahag Stahl, etc., 1983
The plaintiffs in London accepted by telex an offer made by the defendants in Vienna. Where was the contract made?

Held: (HL) The contract was made in Vienna since in the case of instantaneous communications that was where the acceptance was received. [1983] 2 A.C. 34

Commentary
(1) However, Lord Wilberforce stated that in deciding whether the normal rule should apply the courts should take into account: the intentions of the parties; sound business practice; and sometimes decide where the risks should lie.
(2) See also *The Brimnes* (1975) (see p. 13) on termination of an offer by telex.

Key Principle: **Where the post is used an acceptance is effectively communicated on posting.**

Household Fire Insurance v. Grant 1879
The defendant offered to buy shares in the plaintiff company. The company posted a letter accepting the offer. The letter never

arrived, but the defendant's name was entered as a shareholder. Was the defendant bound to pay the balance due on the shares?

Held: (CA) As soon as the letter of acceptance is posted there is a binding contract, even if the letter is lost or delayed. The post office acts as the agent for both parties. (1879) 4 Ex. D. 216

Commentary
The postal rule can be excluded by the terms of the offer (*e.g. Holwell Securities v. Hughes* (1974) (see p. 16). A postal acceptance can prevail over a revocation of an offer posted earlier (*Byrne v. Van Tienhoven* (1880) (see p. 13).

Key Principle: **For the postal rule to apply it must be reasonable to use the post to accept the offer.**

Quenerduaine v. Cole 1883
D made an offer by telegram, P purported to accept by letter.

Held: It was not reasonable to use the post to reply to a telegram, and so the acceptance was only effectively communicated when it was received. (1883) 32 W.R. 185

Commentary
The decision is also applicable to offers made by instantaneous means of communication.

Prescribed Mode of Acceptance

Key Principle: **Silence cannot normally be prescribed as a mode of acceptance.**

Felthouse v. Bindley 1862
The plaintiff offered to buy his nephew's horse and wrote: "If I hear no more . . . I consider the horse is mine." The nephew did not respond although there was evidence that the nephew intended to accept his uncle's offer. Was there a binding contract?

Held: The nephew had not communicated his intention and had not done anything to bind himself, so there was no valid acceptance. (1862) 6 L.T. 157

Key Principle: **Where there is a prescribed method of acceptance it is possible to use another method so long as it is not less advantageous.**

Yates Building Co. Ltd v. Pulleyn Ltd 1975

The plaintiff had the option of purchasing land from the defendants. It was a term of the agreement that the option was exercisable by notice in writing, and that such notice was to be sent "by registered or recorded delivery post". The plaintiffs exercised their option by sending a letter using the ordinary post. Was the letter a valid acceptance? (1975) 119 Sol. J. 370

Held: (CA) In this case the use of registered or recorded delivery was not compulsory. Its use was more advantageous to the plaintiff than to the defendant. What mattered was that the substance of the requirement was fulfilled. Therefore, a binding contract had been concluded.

Certainty

Key Principle: **Where a term is so vague that further agreement is necessary then no contract has been concluded.**

Scammell v. Ouston 1941

The plaintiff ordered a van from the defendant. The balance of the purchase price was to be paid on "hire-purchase terms" over two years. The defendant then refused to supply the van.

Held: (HL) There was no contract because the language was not capable of any definite meaning as there were many kinds of hire purchase agreement, and so the agreement was incomplete. [1941] 1 All E.R. 14

Commentary

(1) Note that the courts will try to find a valid contract where possible and will use various devices such as custom and reasonableness to make sense of a vague term.

(2) In *Baird Textile Holdings Ltd v. Marks & Spencer plc* [2001] EWCA 274 (see also p. 37), the Court of Appeal considered that any obligations imposed on D were insufficiently certain to be terms of a contract because there were no objective criteria by which the court could assess what would be reasonable either as to quantity or price. P had been a principal supplier of garments to D for 30 years when without warning in October 1999, D terminated the arrangement from the end of the current production season. It was accepted that there was no express legally binding contract between P and D. P argued unsuccessfully that either there was an implied contract or that D were estopped from terminating the arrangement without giving reasonable notice.

Key Principle: **A bare agreement to negotiate lacks certainty and is unenforceable.**

Walford v. Miles 1992
The plaintiffs were interested in purchasing the defendants' business. The defendants agreed to terminate negotiations with any third party (a lock-out agreement), and to negotiate only with the plaintiffs. Subsequently they sold the business to a third party. [1992] 2 W.L.R. 174

Held: (HL) The agreement to negotiate was, like an agreement to agree, unenforceable because it lacked certainty. In particular there was no time limit on the negotiations, nor was there any provision for either party to withdraw from them. English law does not recognise a duty to negotiate in good faith.

Key Principle: **The use of the words "subject to contract" means that there is no legally binding contract.**

Regalian Properties Plc v. London Docklands Development Corporation 1995
The plaintiffs offered the defendants £18.5 million "subject to contract" for a licence to build on the defendants' land. The property market then collapsed and it was not financially worthwhile proceeding with the contract. The plaintiffs tried to recover from the defendants the £3 million which they had spent in preparation for the proposed contract.

Held: (Ch D) The words "subject to contract" meant that the loss lay where it fell. The plaintiffs could not recover in restitution (see Chapter 1) because the costs which the plaintiffs incurred did not amount to accelerated performance of the contract, and the decision not to enter into the contract was not made unilaterally by the defendant. [1995] 1 W.L.R. 212

Key Principle: **There is no hard and fast rule whether a letter of intent gives rise to a binding agreement.**

British Steel Corporation v. Cleveland Bridge and Engineering Co. Ltd 1984
(see p. 4).

Held: (QBD) Since the parties had not reached agreement on the price and other essential terms, such as liability for late delivery, there was no binding contract. So the plaintiffs were not liable to pay damages for breach of contract because of the late delivery of one node. However, the defendants were bound to pay a reasonable sum (in restitution) for the manufacture of the nodes as it was done at their request. [1984] 1 All E.R. 504

Key Principle: **Where a subsidiary term of an agreement is left open and is capable of being ascertained then the contract will be upheld.**

Sudbrook Trading Estate Ltd v. Eggleton 1982
The plaintiff tenants gave notice to their landlords that they wanted to exercise an option in their lease to purchase the freehold. The price was to be fixed by two valuers, one nominated by the landlords, and one by the tenants. The landlords refused to nominate a valuer.

Held: (HL) There was a valid contract. The main purpose of the option agreement was the sale of the land at a fair and reasonable price. The price was capable of being ascertained, and the method of ascertaining it was not an essential part of the agreement. [1982] 3 W.L.R. 315

Key Principle: **The fact that a transaction has been performed on both sides will make it difficult to argue that the contract is void for vagueness or uncertainty.**

G Percy Trentham Ltd v. Archital Luxfer Ltd 1993
(see p. 1).

Held: (CA) Where the transaction was fully performed a contract could be concluded by conduct, or come into existence during performance. So there was a legally binding contract. The parties plainly intended to enter into such a contract. [1993] 1 Lloyd's Rep. 25

Commentary
Cf. BSC v. Cleveland Bridge and Engineering Co. Ltd (1984).

3. CONSIDERATION

Introduction—Past Consideration
Adequacy—Sufficiency
Promissory Estoppel—Other Exceptions

Introduction

Key Principle: **For a promise to be enforceable as a contract some consideration must be given in exchange for the promise, that is the promisor must receive a benefit or the promisee must suffer a detriment.**

Currie v. Misa 1875
P sued D on a cheque given to pay off a pre-existing debt. D argued that P had not provided fresh consideration for the debt.

Held: P was entitled to the money. (1875) L.R. 10 Ex. 153

Commentary
(1) This case is important because of the following definition of consideration given by the court of first instance. "A valuable

consideration, in the sense of the law, may consist either in some right, interest, profit or benefit accruing to one party or some forbearance, detriment, loss or responsibility, given suffered or undertaken by the other."

(2) Since *Williams v. Roffey* (1991) (see p. 29) a factual benefit or detriment is sufficient.

(3) Many of the cases in this chapter are concerned with an agreed variation or termination of an existing contract, which normally requires accord (agreement) and satisfaction (consideration) to be legally binding. See discharge by agreement (Chapter 12).

(4) The decision on the precise facts has been replaced by section 27 of the Bills Of Exchange Act 1882.

Key Principle: **Consideration must move from the promisee.**

Tweddle v. Atkinson 1861
The father of the bride and the father of the bridegroom agreed with each other that they would both pay a sum of money to the bridegroom on account of the marriage. They further agreed that the bridegroom should be able to sue either of them if they failed to pay. The bride's father died without paying the money and the bridegroom Tweddle sued his father-in-law's executor for the money.

Held: Tweddle, the promisee, had not provided consideration for his father-in-law's promise. Therefore, he could not enforce the promise. [1861–1873] All E.R. Rep. 369

Commentary
The court further stated that natural love and affection is not valid consideration. The decision is also authority for the doctrine of privity of contract (see p. 42).

Past Consideration

Key Principle: **Past consideration is not good consideration**

Re McArdle 1951
Adult children were entitled to their mother's house after her death. One of the children and his wife lived in the house with

his mother. The wife carried out certain improvements to the house. Subsequently all the children promised to pay her a sum of money when the house was eventually sold to recompense her for the money she had spent on the improvements.

Held: (CA) The wife had not provided consideration in exchange for the children's promise, because the improvements had been completed before the promise was made. [1951] Ch. 669

Commentary
(1) The children's promise was subsequent to and independent of the improvements being carried out.
(2) Executory and executed consideration are regarded as good consideration.

Key Principle: **If the act was done or promise made at the request of the promisor, and it was understood that payment would be made, then the promise to pay is enforceable.**

Pao On v. Lau Yiu Long 1979
As part of a larger agreement the plaintiffs promised not to sell 2.5 million of the 4.2 million shares they owned in a company controlled by the defendants. Subsequently the defendants agreed to buy back 2.5 million shares at a fixed price. The plaintiffs then realised that this was a bad bargain because the price was fixed at $2.50 even if the value of the shares rose. So the plaintiffs refused to proceed with the first agreement unless the defendants cancelled the second agreement and replaced it by an indemnity which guaranteed a minimum price of $2.50 per share. The defendants provided the indemnity which also referred to the plaintiffs promise in the first agreement not to sell the shares. The value of the shares fell and the plaintiffs claimed the money due under the indemnity.

Held: (JCPC) It was understood at the time of the first agreement that the plaintiff's promise not to sell the shares would be compensated for by the defendants promising to indemnify the plaintiffs against any fall in the price of the shares. Therefore, the subsequent indemnity was not independent of the original promise, and the consideration for the defendants' promise was good. [1980] A.C. 614

Commentary
This case is also concerned with sufficiency of consideration (see p. 28) and economic duress (see p. 108).

Adequacy of Consideration

Key Principle: **Consideration need not be adequate.**

Chappell & Co. Ltd v. Nestlé Co. Ltd 1960
The defendant chocolate manufacturers sold a record to the public in return for money and three chocolate bar wrappers. The plaintiffs owned the copyright of the record. They were entitled to a royalty calculated by reference to the "ordinary retail selling price", which the defendants claimed was the money payment alone, and did not include the wrappers.

Held: (HL) The chocolate wrappers formed part of the consideration. They had some economic value because they induced people to buy chocolate which they might otherwise not have bought. [1959] 3 W.L.R. 168

Commentary
Adequate in this context means reasonable or proportionate.

Sufficiency of Consideration

Key Principle: **Consideration must be of some economic value.**

White v. Bluett 1853
A son promised not to bore his father with his complaints if his father did not sue him on a promissory note.

Held: The son's promise had no economic value and so the son had provided no consideration for his father's promise. (1853) 23 L.J. Ex. 36

Commentary
Sufficiency of consideration means that the consideration must have some economic value. This issue arises firstly in relation to the performance of an existing duty and secondly in relation to a creditor accepting a smaller amount of money than that due under the contract.

Performance of an Existing Duty

Key Principle: **A promise to do something which you are already bound to do under the general law is not good consideration.**

Collins v. Godefroy 1831
Godefroy was the plaintiff in a case in which Godefroy promised to pay the witness, Collins, six guineas as an attendance fee. Collins had been ordered by the court to give evidence.

Held: Collins had not provided consideration for Godefroy's promise. (1831) 1 B. & Ad. 950

Key Principle: **A promise to do more than you are already bound to do under the general law is good consideration.**

Glasbrook Bros v. Glamorgan County Council 1925
The police, at the request of a colliery owner, stationed police continuously at his mine during industrial action by the miners.

Held: (HL) The police went beyond the duty imposed upon them by the general law to provide protection, and so provided consideration for the colliery owner's promise to pay them. [1925] A.C. 270

Commentary
If there is any suggestion that the promise to pay has been induced by, for example, extortion or corruption then the court is unlikely to find that consideration has been provided.

Key Principle: **A promise to do something that you are already bound to do under an existing contract with the promisee is not good consideration.**

Stilk v. Myrick 1809
Stilk, a seaman, signed up for a voyage from London to the Baltic and back. During the voyage two seaman deserted. The master of the ship agreed to divide their pay between the

remaining members of the crew if they would work the ship
back to London without the two deserters being replaced. On
their return the master refused to pay Stilk and the other
seamen.

Held: Stilk and the other seamen had not provided any
consideration for the master's promise. They merely agreed to
do what they were already bound to do. (1809) 170 All E.R. Rep.
851.

Commentary
(1) The court was also concerned that seamen would be able to
hold their masters to ransom if the master's promise was enforceable. The principle of economic duress would now provide an
alternative ground for holding a promise invalid in such
circumstances.
(2) This decision can now be distinguished in most cases so that
the principle is of little practical importance (see the next three
cases).

Key Principle: **A promise to do more than you are already
bound to do under the original contract is good consideration.**

Pinnel's Case 1602
Cole owed Pinnel £8.50 which was due to be paid on November
11, 1600. At Pinnel's request Cole paid £5.11 on October 1, 1600,
in full satisfaction of the debt.

Held: In principle, payment of a lesser sum before the date
due is good consideration. However, because of a defect in the
defendant's pleadings Pinnel was able to recover the balance.
(1602) 5 Co. Rep. 117a

Commentary
(1) The court stated that payment of a lesser sum in satisfaction of
a greater sum is generally not good consideration (see *Foakes v.
Beer* 1884, *et seq.*, p. 30).
(2) The court also considered that payment at a different place
than that originally agreed, or payment in kind such as "the gift of
a horse, hawk, robe" would be good consideration.

Key Principle: **Where you are legally entitled to refuse to perform the original contract, then a promise to do something that you were bound to do under that contract is good consideration.**

Hartley v. Ponsonby 1857

The plaintiff, an able seaman, signed up with the master of a ship for a voyage from London to Australia and back. There was a crew of 36, but 17 of them deserted on arrival in Australia. The master agreed to pay the plaintiff £40 if he helped to sail the ship to Bombay with the remaining crew.

Held: The plaintiff's original contract was terminated because it was dangerous to sail the ship with a crew of 19 men. Therefore, the plaintiff had entered into a new contract and had to provide good consideration for the master's promise. (1857) 7 El. & Bl. 872

Commentary

£40 was not regarded an exorbitant sum in the circumstances.

Key Principle: **If the promisee obtains a benefit or avoids a detriment from the performance of a promise, that is good consideration, even if the promisor was already bound to perform the promise under an existing contract with the promisee.**

Williams v. Roffey Bros & Nicholls (Contractors) Ltd 1990

The defendant building contractors were refurbishing a block of flats for the owners. They sub-contracted the carpentry work to the plaintiff. The plaintiff started the work but ran into financial difficulties and there was a risk that they would not complete the job. Under the main contract the defendants were liable to pay a financial penalty if the refurbishment was not completed on time. The defendants agreed to pay an additional sum of money per flat to the plaintiff if they completed the work on time.

Held: (CA) The plaintiff could recover the additional sum. The defendants received a practical benefit because the work was completed on time, and they did not have to engage another sub-contractor. [1991] 1 Q.B. 1

Commentary
(1) The plaintiff did not incur a "legal" detriment nor did the defendants receive a "legal" benefit because the plaintiff did not carry out any work in addition to that agreed under the original contract. Factual detriment and benefit would now appear to be good consideration. In most cases a party to a contract would receive a factual benefit if the other party promises to keep their side of the bargain rather than breaching the contract.
(2) There is a narrow line between this case and economic duress (see p. 108). In this case both parties accepted that the price the plaintiffs quoted for the work was too low, but the promisor offered to pay the additional sum of money.

Key Principle: **A promise to perform or the performance of a pre-existing contractual obligation to a third party is good consideration.**

Pao On v. Lau Yiu Long 1979
(For full facts see p. 25). The plaintiffs refused to proceed with an agreement made with a third party (a company controlled by the defendants) unless the defendants cancelled the subsidiary agreement and replaced it by an indemnity which guaranteed a minimum price of $2.50 per share.

Held: (JCPC) The promise to perform the first agreement was good consideration for the defendants' promise to indemnify the plaintiffs. [1980] A.C. 614

Payment of a Lesser Sum

Key Principle: **Payment of a lesser sum by the debtor is not satisfaction for a greater sum.**

Foakes v. Beer 1884
The plaintiff had obtained judgment against the defendant for £2,090. However, she agreed to allow the defendant to pay her by instalments and not to take any proceedings to enforce the judgment. A judgment debt attracts interest from the date of the judgment. The defendant paid the debt, and the plaintiff claimed the interest.

Held: (HL) The plaintiff was entitled to recover the interest. Even if the plaintiff had agreed to forgo the interest the defendant had not provided any consideration for such a promise. [1881–1885] All E.R. Rep. 106

Commentary
(1) The court applied *Pinnel's Case* (1602) (see p. 28).
(2) "Satisfaction" means "consideration" in this context.

Key Principle: **Even where it is beneficial to the creditor to be paid a lesser sum this will still not be satisfaction for the greater sum.**

Re Selectmove Ltd 1995
A company owed money to the Inland Revenue. The company promised to pay off its existing and future debts by instalments. The Inland Revenue sought to have the company wound up and to recover the debt due.

Held: (CA) The company's promise did not constitute good consideration, even if there was a practical advantage to the Inland Revenue in that they were more likely to recover the money by accepting payment by instalments. [1995] 1 W.L.R 474

Commentary
(1) *Foakes v. Beer* (1884) applied, with some regret.
(2) *Williams v. Roffey* (1991) distinguished. The principle in *Williams v. Roffey & Nicholls* (see p. 29) applied to a contract for the supply of goods and services, but should not be extended to an obligation to pay money such as that arising in *Foakes v. Beer*. Is this logical?
(3) The court decided that on the facts the company could not successfully raise the defence of promissory estoppel (see below).

Key Principle: **Payment of a lesser sum by a third party is treated as satisfaction for a greater sum.**

Hirachand Punamchand v. Temple 1911
A father wrote offering to pay a proportion of his son's debt in full settlement of the whole debt. The plaintiff creditor cashed the banker's draft enclosed with the father's letter.

Held: (CA) The plaintiff could not recover the balance from the son. [1911] 2 K.B. 330

Commentary
(1) The main reason for the decision is that it would be a fraud upon a third party to the original contract if the creditor was allowed to recover the balance from the debtor. No consideration is given by the debtor for the creditor's promise.
(2) Fraud (on the other creditors) is also the reason why compositions with creditors are upheld, even though the debtor has not provided any consideration for his creditors agreeing between themselves to accept, e.g. 10 per cent of what the debtor owes each of them.

Promissory Estoppel

Key Principle: **Where A makes a promise to B which is intended to be binding and to be acted upon, and is in fact acted upon, then A is bound by the promise even where B has provided no consideration for it.**

Central London Property Trust Ltd v. High Trees House Ltd 1947

In 1937 the plaintiff granted the defendant a 99–year lease of a block of flats at a rent of £2,500 a year. When the Second World War broke out in September 1939 the defendant had not fully sub-let all the flats, and so was unable to pay the annual rent. The plaintiff agreed that the rent should be halved as from the beginning of the lease. By the beginning of 1945 the flats were fully let. The plaintiff initially claimed all the arrears, but the case was heard on the basis that the full rent should be paid from July 1945.

Held: (KBD) The plaintiff was entitled to the full rent as from July 1945. By then the conditions prevailing when the promise was made, had completely passed away. If the plaintiff had claimed the balance of the rent for the war years, Denning J. stated that they would not have succeeded. [1947] K.B. 130

Commentary
(1) Denning J. established the equitable principle of promissory estoppel by fusing two existing equitable principles: estoppel by representation; and equitable waiver (see *Hughes v. Metropolitan*

Railway (1877)). This enabled him to avoid having to follow the principle of *Foakes v. Beer* (see p. 30).

(2) There must be a clear and unambiguous promise for the principle to apply.

(3) This decision is a major landmark in the law of contract because a promise was enforced even though no consideration was given for it. However, its importance may be reduced because of the wider definition of consideration accepted in *Williams v. Roffey* (see p. 29).

Key Principle: **Promissory estoppel can only be used as a defence, not as a cause of action.**

Combe v. Combe 1951

A wife obtained a divorce (decree nisi) from her husband, who then promised to pay her £100 a year as a maintenance payment. So the wife did not apply to the court for maintenance payments. The divorce was finalised (decree absolute). The husband never paid the wife any maintenance and she sued him on his promise.

Held: (CA) The wife could not enforce the promise. She had provided no consideration and promissory estoppel merely prevented a party from insisting upon their strict legal rights, when it would be unjust to allow them to do so. Promissory estoppel should be used as "a shield not as a sword". [1951] 1 All E.R. 767

Commentary

(1) In *Baird Textile Holdings Ltd v. Marks & Spencer plc* [2001] EWCA 274 (see p. 21) the Court of Appeal confirmed that promissory estoppel and estoppel by convention merely provide defences to a claim. They do not establish enforceable obligations, although Judge L.J. considered that the House of Lords might review this limitation in the future.

(2) Compare with proprietary estoppel which may be used as a 'sword'. In *Gillett v. Holt* [2000] 3 W.L.R. 815; [2000] 2 All E.R. 289, the Court of Appeal held that detrimental reliance on a promise to leave a farming business to the appellant on the respondent's death made the promise irrevocable and enforceable by the appellant.

(3) Note that proprietary as opposed to promissory estoppel arises where a promise is made as to future rights over land. The promisor is estopped from going back on the promise where the promisee has relied on the promise to his detriment.

Key Principle: **A promise to suspend payments operates until the creditor gives reasonable notice of their intention to resume their strict legal rights.**

Tool Metal Manufacturing Co. Ltd v. Tungsten Electric Co. Ltd 1955

In 1937 the appellants (TMMC) licensed the respondents to trade in hard metal alloys. The appellants were entitled to be paid compensation if, for example, the respondents used more than a certain amount of alloys in any month. The respondents paid the compensation until the outbreak of war in 1939, when the appellants agreed to suspend the payments on the understanding that a new agreement would be negotiated to come into effect at the end of the war. Negotiations broke down in 1944, and in March 1945 the appellants claimed compensation under the original agreement as from June 1, 1945. The case reached the Court of Appeal which held that although the agreement in 1939 was to suspend not to end the payments, the appellants had not given reasonable notice to the respondents of their intention that the compensation payments be resumed. The appellants then started another action claiming compensation as from January 1, 1947, reasonable notice of their claim having been given in March 1945.

Held: (HL) Reasonable notice had now been given and the appellants were entitled to the payments agreed under the 1937 licence agreement. [1955] 1 W.L.R. 761

Commentary

The principle of equitable waiver (*Hughes v. Metropolitan Railway* (1877)) was the basis of the decision, but the key principle also applies to promissory estoppel.

Key Principle: **The promise only becomes final and irrevocable if the promisee cannot resume their position.**

Ajayi v. Briscoe 1964
The plaintiff sued the defendant to recover instalments due under an agreement to hire purchase 11 lorries. The defendant pleaded promissory estoppel on the ground that the plaintiff had agreed to accept the suspension of the payments until certain conditions were fulfilled.

Held: (JCPC) The defendant was not successful because he was unable to prove that the conditions had not been fulfilled. [1964] 1 W.L.R. 1326

Commentary
Lord Hodson stated that the doctrine of promissory estoppel is subject to three qualifications:

(1) the promisee should have altered their position in reliance on the promise;

(2) the promisor can go back on their promise on the giving of reasonable notice (see above); and

(3) the promise only becomes final and irrevocable if the promisee cannot resume their position.

Key Principle: **The promisee need not have relied on the promise to their detriment, the question is whether it would be inequitable to allow the promisor to enforce their rights.**

The Post Chaser 1982
The buyers of palm oil re-asserted their contractual right to reject the oil two days after promising not to do so. The sellers subsequently sold the oil at a loss.

Held: It was not inequitable to allow the buyers to assert their strict contractual rights. [1982] 1 All E.R. 19

Commentary
Robert Goff J. also found that the promisee had not suffered any prejudice or detriment. Would it have made a difference if they had?

Key Principle: **The promise must have been given with full consent, not extracted by threats from the promisee.**

D & C Builders v. Rees 1966

The plaintiffs were a small firm of builders. They were owed £482 for some work which they had done for the defendant. After making several requests to be paid the plaintiffs were offered £300 in full satisfaction of the debt. The defendant stated that it was £300 or nothing. The plaintiffs reluctantly accepted £300 because they were close to bankruptcy. Subsequently, the plaintiffs sued for the balance.

Held: (CA) The plaintiffs were not estopped from claiming the balance because they did not voluntarily accept the lesser sum. [1966] 2 W.L.R. 288.

Commentary

The defendant paid by cheque rather than by cash. The court rejected the defendant's argument that payment by cheque introduced a new element and amounted to consideration for the plaintiff's promise.

4. INTENTION TO CREATE LEGAL RELATIONS

Mere Puffs

Key Principle: **Mere puffs are statements which are not intended to be taken seriously and which have no legal effect.**

Lambert v. Lewis 1981

A manufacturer stated in promotional literature their product, a towing hitch, was "foolproof" and that it "required no maintenance".

Held: These statements were not promises which could give rise to a contract between the manufacturer and a dealer, because they were not intended to be terms of a contract. [1981] 1 All E.R. 1185

Commentary
In *Carlill v. Carbolic Smoke Ball Co* (see p. 7) D claimed unsuccessfully that the advertisement was a mere puff.

Presumptions
Commercial Agreements

Key Principle: **The presumption that parties to a commercial agreement intend to create legal relations can be rebutted by an "honour clause".**

Rose and Frank Co. v. J R Crompton 1923
In 1913 P & D agreed in writing that D would supply paper tissues to P. Prices were quoted for six-month periods. However a clause provided: "This arrangement is not entered into, nor is this memorandum written, as a formal or legal agreement, and shall not be subject to legal jurisdiction in the law courts . . ." In 1919 D terminated the arrangement. P sued for breach of contract and non-delivery of goods.

Held: (HL) The arrangement of 1913 was not a binding contract. Nevertheless, each order accepted was a binding contract. There was no reason why even in business matters, the parties should not intend to rely on an honourable understanding, however they should express themselves so precisely that outsiders have no difficulty in understanding what they mean. [1925] 2 A.C. 445

Commentary
(1) HL adopted the reasoning of Atkin L.J. in CA.
(2) Similar provisions are found in football pool coupons (*e.g. Jones v. Vernon's Pools* (1938)).
(3) In *Baird Textile Holdings v. Marks & Spencer plc* (see p. 21) the Court of Appeal considered that the lack of certainty as to the parties' obligations confirmed the absence of any clear evidence of an intention to create legal relations.

Key Principle: **The onus of rebutting the presumption rests on the party claiming that it does not apply.**

Edwards v. Skyways Ltd 1964

D airline agreed with British Airline Pilots Association to pay *"ex gratia"* payments "approximating to" an easily calculated sum to pilots made redundant. P, a pilot, sued for such a payment under the agreement. D claimed that there was no intention to create legal relations and that the promise was too vague.

Held: (QBD) It was a commercial agreement. Therefore the presumption was that there was an intention to create legal relations. The onus was on D to rebut the presumption which they had not done. The use of words *"ex gratia"* merely meant that D did not admit any *pre-existing* liability, rather than there was no legally binding agreement. [1964] 1 W.L.R. 349

Key Principle: **If there is any doubt about whether the presumption should apply then the court should use an objective test to decide the issue.**

Esso Petroleum Ltd v. Commissioners of Customs and Excise 1976

In 1970 garage owners selling Esso petrol offered a "free" World Cup coin with every four gallons of petrol bought. The coins were of little intrinsic value. P claimed that the coins were chargeable to tax because they were "produced in quantity for general sale."

Held: (HL) There was no "sale" of the coins. On the question of whether the coins were the subject-matter of a contract between the garage owner and a motorist, three judges held that there was an intention to create legal relations because:

(1) Esso's advertising literature was produced for commercial advantage;

(2) it was generally undesirable to allow commercial promoters to claim that statements were mere puffs; and

(3) precedent supported this view. [1976] 1 W.L.R. 1

Commentary

Two judges held that there was no intention to create legal relations because:

(1) it was not necessary for the success of the scheme for garage owners to subject themselves to contractual liability;

(2) the coins were trivial and of little value; and

(3) garage owners were unlikely to renege, because it was not in their interest to do so.

Key Principle: **The court should look at the totality of the evidence in deciding whether the presumption is rebutted.**

J Evans, etc., v. Andrea Merzario Ltd 1976

D proposed that in future D would ship P's goods in containers. D's representative gave an oral assurance that the containers would be shipped below deck not on deck and on this basis P agreed to D's proposal. Subsequently, a container was placed on deck by mistake, and was not properly fastened down. The container fell overboard and was lost.

Held: (CA) D's oral assurance even though it was made during a courtesy call was intended to be legally binding. It was clear from all the evidence that P only agreed to the use of containers because of D's promise that they would be carried below deck. [1976] 1 W.L.R. 1078

Domestic and Social Arrangements

Key Principle: **There is a presumption that in arrangements between husband and wife the parties do not intend to create legal relations.**

Balfour v. Balfour 1919

D, the husband, worked in Ceylon. P, his wife, had to stay in England for medical reasons. D agreed to pay P £30 a month. P and D subsequently separated. P sued D for money owing under their agreement.

Held: (CA) P could not recover the money because such arrangements are not usually intended to be legally binding. If they were it would result in a flood of litigation. Domestic affairs should be dealt with privately. [1919] 2 K.B. 571

Key Principle: **The presumption is rebutted where the parties have separated or are about to separate when they enter into the arrangement.**

Merritt v. Merritt 1970

D, the husband, left the matrimonial home, which was in the joint names of D and P his wife. Subsequently D and P agreed that D would pay P £40 a month, out of which P should pay the mortgage. D signed an agreement that in return for P paying off the mortgage, he would transfer his share of the property to P once the mortgage was paid off.

Held: (CA) P could enforce D's promise. Looking at the situation objectively parties who are no longer happily married clearly intend any agreement to be legally binding. [1970] 1 W.L.R. 1211

Key Principle: **Where a party gives up legal rights in reliance upon a domestic arrangement the arrangement is legally binding.**

Tanner v. Tanner 1975

P, a married man, promised D, a single woman, that she and their two young children would be able to live in a house purchased by P until the children left school. D, in reliance on this promise moved out of her rent-controlled flat. The relationship ended. P claimed possession of the house.

Held: (CA) D had a contractual licence to live in the house purchased by P, so long as the children were of school age and accommodation was reasonably required for her and the children. [1975] 1 W.L.R. 1346

Key Principle: **There is a presumption that in family arrangements the parties do not intend to create legal relations.**

Jones v. Padavatton 1969

P, a mother, offered D, her daughter, an allowance if D gave up her job in the United States and came to London to study for the Bar. D did so. Two years later P bought a house in London for D to live in and so that D could have an income from renting out spare rooms. Three years later P claimed possession of the house. D had not yet passed the Bar exams.

Held: (CA) The mother and daughter were very close when the agreement was made. There was no intention to create legal relations. The arrangement was vague and uncertain. [1969] 1 W.L.R. 328

Commentary

(1) In a dissenting judgment Salmon L.J. held that there was an intention to be legally bound. However, the agreement was only to last until the studies were completed. The implication was that they would be completed within a reasonable time.

(2) In *Hardwick v. Johnson* (1978) where a mother bought a house for her son and daughter-in-law, who paid her £7.00 a week towards the purchase price, the court held that the son and daughter-in-law had a contractual licence.

Key Principle: **An arrangement between members of the same household can rebut the presumption.**

Simpkins v. Pays 1955

Three ladies, two of whom were related, lived in the same house. Every week they jointly took part in a newspaper fashion competition. They agreed to pool their entries and to share any prize money. The entry was always sent in D's name.

Held: (QBD) P could recover one third of the prize money from D. There was an intention to be legally bound. [1955] 1 W.L.R. 975

Commentary

Presumably the same approach would be adopted whether or not they lived in the same house, and would also apply to lottery winnings.

5. PRIVITY OF CONTRACT

Key Principle: **Contractual rights and duties can only be conferred or imposed on the parties to a contract.**

Tweddle v. Atkinson 1861
P's father and his prospective father-in-law promised to pay P a sum of money on his marriage. His father-in-law died. P sued D, his father-in-law's personal representative, for the money.

Held: P could not recover the money. He was neither a party to the contract nor had he provided consideration for his father-in-law's promise. He could not be sued on the contract, therefore he should not be able to sue on it. [1861—1873] All E.R. Rep. 369

Commentary
(1) There is dispute as to whether the key principle is merely a consequence of the rule that consideration must move from the promisee (see p. 24).
(2) This case is the starting point for the doctrine of privity. Older cases dating from the seventeenth century had considered that a third party could enforce a contract made for their benefit.

Who are the Parties to the Contract?

Key Principle: **A collateral contract may enable a person who is not a party to the main contract to enforce that contract.**

Shanklin Pier v. Detel Products Ltd 1951
P employed X to paint P's pier and instructed X to buy and use paint made by D. P relied on a representation made by D that the paint would last seven years. In fact it only lasted three months. X purchased the paint from D.

Held: (KBD) A collateral contract existed between P and D; its main term was that the paint would last seven years. [1951] 2 All E.R. 471

Commentary
(1) It is usually straightforward to ascertain who are the parties to a contract. However, where agents are and/or companies are involved it can be problematic.

(2) Today the plaintiff could possibly sue in tort for negligent misstatement (*Hedley Byrne v. Heller* (1964)).

The Essentials of the Doctrine

Key Principle: **Only a person who is a party to a contract can sue on it.**

Dunlop Pneumatic Tyre Co. Ltd v. Selfridge & Co. Ltd 1915

P sold tyres to X on the basis that X would not resell them at less than P's list price, and that if X resold the tyres to trade buyers X would extract a similar undertaking from them. X sold tyres to D who agreed to the undertakings, and also agreed to pay P £5 for each tyre sold in breach. D supplied two tyres in breach of the undertaking. P sued for two sums of £5 as liquidated damages. P was not a party to the contract between X and D.

Held: (HL) P could not recover the liquidated damages. Lord Haldane stated: "In the law of England certain principles are fundamental. One is that only a person who is a party to a contract can sue on it." [1967] 3 W.L.R. 932

Commentary

Lord Dunedin: (1) Concentrated on whether the plaintiff had provided any consideration for the defendant's undertaking.
(2) Considered that it would be possible for the plaintiff to have framed the agreement so as to bind the defendant.

Key Principle: **The remedy of specific performance may enable a contract to be enforced for the benefit of a third party.**

Beswick v. Beswick 1968

P's husband was a coal merchant. He transferred his business to D, his nephew, in return for which D agreed to pay P an annuity of £5 per week in the event of her husband's death. After P's husband died D paid P £5 once. P sued D for arrears and for specific performance of the agreement. P sued in two capacities: (1) as widow; (2) as administrator of her husband's estate.

Held: (HL) P could not succeed as "widow", because she was a third party to the agreement. However, P could succeed as "administrator" (*i.e.* in place of deceased husband). An order of specific performance was granted. [1967] 3 W.L.R. 932

Commentary
(1) P as "administrator" could not recover damages from D because under the agreement the money was not payable to P as administrator, and the estate had suffered no loss so only nominal damages would be recoverable.
(2) Lord Reid considered that P's inability to recover the money as "widow" could mean that the law is sadly deficient.

Damages for Third Party's Losses

Key Principle: **As a general rule where X makes a contract with Y for the benefit of Z then X cannot recover damages for Z's losses.**

Woodar Investment Development Ltd v. Wimpey Construction (U.K.) Ltd 1980
D agreed to buy land from P. Subsequently D purported to cancel the agreement. The main question was whether D were entitled to do so. If they were not then P could claim damages. Part of the purchase price would have been paid to X, a third party. Could P recover damages on behalf of X?

Held: (HL) D was entitled to terminate the agreement. Even if they had not been so entitled, P could not have recovered damages on behalf of X. [1980] 1 W.L.R. 277

Key Principle: **In certain types of contract where X makes a contract with Y for the benefit of Z then X can recover damages for Z's losses.**

Jackson v. Horizon Holidays 1975
P booked a holiday in Sri Lanka for himself, his wife and his two children. The accommodation and facilities did not correspond with what had been promised by D.

Held: P could recover damages for the whole family's disappointment and inconvenience as well as for his own. [1975] 1 W.L.R. 1468

Commentary
This principle has been restricted to holiday contracts and similar social activities undertaken by a group: *Woodar Investment Ltd v. Wimpey* (1980) (see above).

Key Principle: **Where there is a contract for a large development of property which to both parties' knowledge is going to be occupied, etc., by a third party then the assignor can recover damages for the third party's losses.**

Linden Gardens Trust v. Lenesta Sludge Disposals 1993

St Martin's Property Corpn Ltd v. Sir Robert McAlpine & Sons Ltd 1993
These two cases were heard together.
In *Linden Gardens*, X, a lessee, entered into two contracts with D for the removal of asbestos from the leased building. Soon after the contracts had been performed X assigned the lease to P, and assigned their rights under the two contracts. P paid the market price for the lease as it was thought, wrongly in fact, that all the asbestos had been removed. X suffered no loss, and were removed as a party to the proceedings. In *St Martin's*, P1 assigned at full value a building development to P2, and also assigned the benefit of the building contract. The breach of the building contract had not yet occurred. In both cases there were express prohibitions against the assignment of the benefit of the contracts without both parties' consent. This consent was not obtained. P sued D for breaches of the assigned contracts.

Held: (HL) The contractual prohibitions against assignment were valid. Therefore in the *Linden Gardens* case P, the assignee, could not sue on the contract. However, in the *St Martin's* case because the assignor P1 was a party to the claim and the nature of the contract was different, *i.e* a large property development intended for third party occupation, P1 would be able to recover damages from D for the loss suffered by P2. [1993] 3 W.L.R. 408

Commentary
The key principle derives from the reasoning of the majority of their Lordships, which is described as "the narrower ground".

Lord Griffiths in the *St Martin's* case reached his decision on what has become known as "the broader ground". He held that the employer under a building contract (P1) may in principle recover substantial damages from a building contractor (D), because he has not received the performance which he was entitled to receive from the contractor under the contract. The implications of "the broader approach" were examined in detail in *Alfred McAlpine Construction Ltd v. Panatown Ltd* [2001] A.C. 518 (see below).

Key Principle: **Where there is a contract for the development of property which is entered into for the benefit of a third party, who was subsequently assigned the benefit of the contract, then the assignee can recover damages for losses caused by a breach of the contract.**

Darlington Borough Council v. Wiltshier Northern Ltd 1995
D a building contractor entered into a contract with X, a finance company, to build a leisure centre for and on land owned by P. X then assigned all its rights under the building contract to P. P claimed that there were serious defects in the leisure centre due to defective workmanship by D.

Held: (CA) P was entitled to recover damages for defects in the performance of the contract. X could not enforce the contract. The established doctrine deprived P of a remedy and allowed the contract-breaker to go scot-free. However, the present case was covered by an exception to the general rule that a plaintiff could only recover damages for his own loss. [1995] 1 W.L.R. 68

Commentary
(1) Steyn L.J. considered that there was no doctrinal, logical or policy reason why the law should deny effectiveness to a contract for the benefit of a third party where that was the expressed intention of the parties.

Key Principle: **A party to a contract (P), for the development of property for the benefit of a third party (X), may not recover damages from the other party to the contract (M) for losses**

suffered by a third party (X) where the other party (M) has entered into a separate duty of care deed with the third party.

Alfred McAlpine Construction Ltd v. Panatown Ltd 2001

M agreed with P to construct a building and a car park on land owned by X, the third party, which was part of the same group of companies as P. M also entered into a duty of care deed with X, whereby X had a direct remedy against M, for failure to exercise reasonable care and skill in the performance of the contract with P. Serious defects were found in the building constructed by M., and X suffered financial loss as a consequence of this breach of contract by M. P suffered no loss but, as a party to the contract with M, sought to recover from M the loss suffered by X.

Held: (HL) P could not recover damages from M for the loss suffered by X. P could only recover damages for loss that he himself has suffered. This case did not fall within the building contracts exception. The duty of care deed was part of a package of arrangements agreed upon by the parties to the main building contract. This package reflected the intention of all the parties that the third party should have a direct cause of action which should exclude any substantial claim by the employer P. [2001] 1 A.C. 518.

Commentary

(1) Lords Clyde, Jauncey and Browne-Wilkinson allowed the appeal by M. Lord Clyde, however, considered that the law should generally permit a contracting party to recover damages for the actual loss that he and a third party has suffered. Lord Browne-Wilkinson considered that allowing P to recover for loss suffered by X without P being liable to account to X for the damages recovered would be "another piece of legal nonsense".

(2) Lords Goff and Millett (dissenting) dismissed M's appeal. They held that privity of contract was not the issue, and based their decision on the broader ground advanced by Lord Griffith's in the *St Martin's* case. Lord Goff considered that their Lordships should be concerned with the rights conferred on P by the main building contract, and that fuller recognition is required of the importance of protecting a contracting party's interests in the performance of the contract. Secondly, their Lordships considered that the duty of care deed made between M and X did not exclude P from pursuing their remedy under the main contract. Lord Goff stated that it was implicit in the contract between P and X that if P

recovered damages from M they would finance the cost to P of remedying the defects in the building.

(3) The contract was made between P and M rather than X and M in order to minimise VAT liability.

(4) The legal position in the building cases is fundamentally affected by the Contracts (Rights of Third Parties) Act 1999. The Act did not apply to these cases because the facts arose before the Act came into force.

Exclusion Clauses and Third Parties

Key Principle: **A third party to a contract can rely on an exclusion clause in a contract made between A and B which protects third parties where A purports to act as agent for the third party.**

New Zealand Shipping Company Ltd v. Satterthwaite & Co. Ltd, The Eurymedon 1974

A, who was sending machinery to P in New Zealand by ship, entered into a transportation contract with B the carrier. D, stevedores in New Zealand, agreed with B to unload the goods on arrival. D negligently unloaded and damaged the machinery. A's rights under the contract having been transferred to P, P sued D. D claimed that they were entitled to the protection of the exclusion clause in the contract between A and B. The complex clause stated that no servant or agent (including any independent contractor (D), employed by the Carrier) of the Carrier (B), shall be under any liability for any loss or damages caused by any negligence on his part while acting in connection with the employment, and that every exclusion clause which protected the Carrier (B) would also protect the carrier's servants and agents (D) on whose behalf the Carrier (B) acted as agent so that D would be treated as a party to the contract between A and B.

Held: (JCPC) D was protected by the exclusion clause and was not liable to P. [1974] 2 W.L.R. 865

Commentary

(1) The exclusion clause amounted to a unilateral offer by A that anyone who was engaged by B to perform any of B's obligations under the contract with A, would be regarded as a party to that contract and would be able to benefit from the exclusion clause. D

accepted that offer by unloading the goods, which was also the consideration for A's promise.

(2) The decision reflected commercial realities.

Key Principle: **A third party to a contract between A and B can be bound by an exclusion clause in that contract where the third party impliedly consents to A making a contract with B on the terms normally current in the trade.**

Morris v. C.W. Martin and Sons Ltd 1965

P sent her mink stole to a furrier (F) for cleaning. F told her he would arrange for the fur to be cleaned by D. F contracted with D (as principal not as P's agent). One of D's employees stole the fur. D's contract conditions excluded D from liability for loss or damage to the goods during processing. P sued D.

Held: (CA) P agreed that F should send her fur to D, and so consented to the exclusion clause. [1965] 3 W.L.R. 276

Commentary

However CA also held that the wording of the exclusion clause did not apply to loss or damage which occurred before or after processing. Therefore the wording of the clause did not cover P's actual loss. (see p. 72).

6. FORMALITIES AND CAPACITY

Key Principle: **An oral contract is legally enforceable except where formalities are required.**

Jayaar Impex Ltd v. Toaken Group Ltd 1996

P agreed to purchase Nigerian gum arabic from D. Agreement was reached in telephone conversations made on October 17 and 19, 1994. D claimed that the terms of the contract were contained in a written contract dated October 21, 1994. A dispute arose as to the quality of the goods. P claimed that they were not bound to comply with the dispute procedures set out in the written contract.

Held: (QBD) The contract was made orally on the telephone. It was final and binding. [1996] 2 Lloyd's Rep. 437

Formalities

The Sale or Disposition of an Interest in Land

Key Principle: **There must be an "exchange of contracts" or one document recording the agreement.**

Commission for the New Towns v. Cooper (Great Britain) Ltd 1995
P and D agreed in a series of letters that D could have an option to require P to take an assignment of a lease from D.

Held: (CA) An offer and acceptance in the course of correspondence does not satisfy the requirements of section 2 of the Law of Property (Miscellaneous Provisions) Act 1989. [1995] 2 W.L.R. 677

Key Principle: **The grant of an option must be signed by both parties to the contract.**

Spiro v. Glencrown Properties Ltd 1991
The plaintiff owner of land granted an option to purchase the property to the defendant. The defendant exercised the option but failed to complete the purchase. Both parties signed the grant of the option, but only the purchaser signed the exercise of the option.

Held: (ChD) The prime purpose of section 2 of the Law of Property (Miscellaneous Provisions) Act 1989 was to record the consent of the parties. The parties consented when the option was granted, and since both parties signed this document, the requirements of section 2 were satisfied and there was a valid contract. [1991] 2 W.L.R. 931

Commentary
Where the subject-matter of the contract is not land, the grant of an option is normally treated as an irrevocable offer which is accepted when the option is exercised. Only then does a valid contract come into effect.

Key Principle: **The interpretation of the word "signed" in section 2 of the new Act should not be encumbered with the ancient baggage of case law on earlier legislation.**

Firstpost Homes Ltd v. Johnson 1995
The owner of land signed a letter and a plan which together set out her agreement to sell the land to the plaintiff. A director of the plaintiff company signed the plan, and the plaintiff's name was typed on the letter as the addressee.

Held: (CA) The letter and not the plan was the document which had to be signed to satisfy the requirements of s.2(3). "Signed" meant a person writing their name with their own hand, it did not include the printing or typing of a name. [1995] 4 All E.R. 355

Commentary
The Court of Appeal considered that the 1989 Act had a different philosophy to the Statute of Frauds and section 40 of the Law of Property Act 1925. Parliament intended that questions as to whether there was a contract and what were its terms, should be answered by looking at a single document.

Key Principle: **Where due to a drafting error the terms of the contract are contained in more than one document, then the court may order rectification of the contract.**

Wright v. Robert Leonard (Developments) Ltd 1994
The plaintiff agreed to buy a show flat together with its fixtures and fittings from the defendant. The exchange of contracts did not take place by the agreed date, and unknown to the plaintiff the defendants removed the furniture before the eventual exchange.

Held: (CA) There was a single contract and all the terms had to be in writing to satisfy section 2, even those relating to the furniture. The contract should be rectified, so that the reference to furniture was included in the written document, and the plaintiff could recover damages from the defendant for breach of contract. [1994] N.P.C. 49

Key Principle: **Where the terms of an agreement are contained in more than one document, then the court may hold that there is a main contract which is subject to section 2 and a collateral contract which is not.**

Record v. Bell 1991
The plaintiff vendor wished to exchange contracts but the relevant Land Registry documents were not yet available. So, in a letter, he gave a warranty as to his title to the defendant purchaser, who then agreed to the exchange of contracts, but subsequently refused to complete the purchase.

Held: (Ch D) The written warranty was an independent contract collateral to the main contract. It was not a contract for the sale of land and was not subject to section 2. The main contract was subject to and complied with section 2. Therefore both contracts were enforceable. [1991] 1 W.L.R. 853

Key Principle: **The formalities required by section 2 also apply to a variation of a term of a contract.**

McCausland v. Duncan Lawrie Ltd 1996
D agreed to sell a property to P. The contract complied with the requirements of section 2, but the date for completion of the purchase was subsequently changed by mutual consent evidenced in correspondence.

Held: (CA) The variation was not signed by both parties and therefore did not comply with section 2. [1996] 4 All E.R. 995

Commentary
Such a variation would have been valid under the previous legislation, but the court re-affirmed that the 1989 Act was intended to effect a major change in the law.

Key principle: **Where a supposed bargain has been fully performed by one side and it would be inequitable to disregard the claimant's expectations the exception in s.2(5) applies.**

Yaxley v. Gott 2001
In 1991 G purchased a house. Y entered into an oral agreement with G whereby Y would convert the house into flats and manage the property in return for becoming the owner of the ground floor flat. In fact the house was purchased by G's son. In 1995 G's son excluded Y from the property.

Held:　(CA) Y was entitled to a long leasehold interest under a constructive trust. [2000] Ch. 162

Commentary
1. Under the Law of Property (Miscellaneous Provisions) Act 1989, s.2(5) a constructive trust is an exception to the normal requirement that such a contract should be in writing.
2. Beldam L.J. considered that s.2(5) also effectively excluded, from the operation of s.2, cases in which an interest in land was claimed by relying on proprietary estoppel. Robert Walker L.J. agreed that the two areas overlap, for example, in the area of a joint enterprise for the acquisition of land.

Guarantees

Key Principle: **An oral contract of guarantee recorded in a note or memorandum signed by the party to be charged is enforceable.**

Elpis Maritime Co v. Marti Chartering Co. (The Maria D) 1991
The plaintiff owners chartered a ship to the charterers. The defendants were brokers for the charterers. Telex and telephone negotiations took place between brokers for both parties, and

the agreement was recorded in a written charterparty, which included a guarantee by the defendants. Subsequently, the plaintiffs were entitled to be paid compensation by the charterers under the terms of the charterparty. The money was not paid and the plaintiffs sought to recover it from the defendants, who claimed that the guarantee was unenforceable because it did not comply with the requirements of section 4 of the Statute of Frauds 1677.

Held: (HL) The contract of guarantee was evidenced in writing as required by section 4 and was enforceable. There was either an oral agreement recorded in the written charterparty which was signed by the defendants, or alternatively the charterparty alone was a sufficient note or memorandum. [1991] 3 W.L.R. 330

Commentary
Section 4 only applies to a contract of guarantee where A promises B that if C does not discharge his liability to B, then A will do so. It does not, for example, apply to a manufacturer's guarantee of their product.

Regulated Consumer Credit and Consumer Hire Agreements

Key principle: **Where a regulated consumer credit agreement is not properly executed, the agreement may not be enforceable by the creditor.**

Dimond v. Lovell 2000
D's car was damaged in a road accident. D hired a replacement car from P, while her car was being repaired. P was a company which hired cars to drivers whose cars had been damaged in accidents caused by another's fault. D did not pay for the hire of the car because part of the agreement was that P would recover the cost of hire from the party at fault.

Held: (HL) The agreement between P and D for the hire of the car was a regulated consumer credit agreement under the Consumer Credit Act 1974, s.65(1). The agreement was unenforceable because it did not contain a term stating the amount of credit provided to D in accordance with regulations made under s.61(1). [2000] 2 All E.R. 897

Key Principle: **Where such an agreement is not properly executed and the consumer suffers prejudice then the court may compensate the consumer.**

National Guardian Mortgage Corp. v. Wilkes 1993
The plaintiff creditor sued the defendant debtor who had failed to keep up repayments on a loan agreement made with the plaintiff. The defendant's house was security for the loan, but the plaintiff in breach of Consumer Credit Act 1974, ss.58(1) and 62(2) had failed to give the defendant an advance copy of the unexecuted loan agreement. This deprived her of the seven-day "consideration period" which she may have used to obtain a loan at a lower rate of interest. The county court judge awarded the defendant compensation under section 127 equivalent to 40 per cent of the interest claimed by the plaintiff.

Held: (CA) The court has a wide discretion and when enforcing an agreement it could compensate the defendant for the prejudice suffered by the defendant and impose such a condition on the creditor under section 136. [1993] C.C.L.R. 1

Key principle: **Primary legislation which prevents a court from enforcing a consumer credit agreement is incompatible with the rights guaranteed to a creditor under the Human Rights Act 1998.**

Wilson v. First County Ltd (No 2) 2001
W entered into a consumer credit agreement with FCL. The amount of the credit was mis-stated in the agreement. This meant that the agreement was not a properly executed regulated agreement, and could only be enforced against the debtor on the order of the court. However, section 127(3) of the Consumer Credit Act 1974 states that the court has no power to make an enforcement order where, as in this case, there is no document signed by the debtor containing all the prescribed terms.

Held: (CA) Section 127(3) was a restriction on the creditor's contractual rights and amounted to a breach of Article 6(1) of the ECHR (entitled to a fair and public hearing by an independent and impartial tribunal in the determination of civil rights) and Article 1 of Protocol 1 (peaceful enjoyment of possessions). The restriction was disproportionate to the policy aims underlying s.127(3). The section could not be interpreted so that it is compatible with Article 6(1). A declaration of incompatibility was made. [2001] 3 W.L.R. 42

Standard Form Contracts

Key Principle: **The courts recognise that standard form contracts can be one-sided but have not developed specific rules to regulate their validity.**

A. Schroeder Music Publishing Co Ltd v. Macaulay 1974

Macaulay, a song-writer entered into a standard form exclusive services contract with the music publishers. (See p. 135 for detailed facts.)

Held: (HL) The contract was void and in restraint of trade. [1974] 1 W.L.R. 1308

Commentary

(1) Lord Diplock identified two types of standard form contract: the first, which are normally fair, are of ancient origin such as bills of lading, and are the result of negotiation between parties of equal bargaining power; and the second, which are of comparatively modern origin, occur where one party is in a superior bargaining position and is able to impose their terms on the weaker party.

(2) Standard form contracts are very common in practice. Although not specifically regulated their terms may be subject to common law principles on restraint of trade, penalty clauses, and incorporation of terms, as well as legislative provisions, for example, the Unfair Contract Terms Act 1977 and the Unfair Terms in Consumer Contracts Regulations 1994.

Capacity

Key Principle: **The contractual capacity of a corporation created by statute is subject to the *ultra vires* doctrine.**

Hazell v. Hammersmith and Fulham London Borough Council 1991

The council entered into a number of "swap agreements" between 1987 and 1989. In essence these agreements enabled the council to gamble on interest rate changes in the money market. If the rates went down the council would make money, but if they went up they would incur losses. The legality of these agreements was questioned by the district auditor when it became apparent that the council was going to incur heavy losses.

Held: (HL) The agreements were void. The council's contractual capacity was limited to the powers conferred on it by statute. The agreements were not incidental to the council's power to borrow money under Local Government Act 1972, s.111. [1991] 2 W.L.R. 372

Commentary
(1) This decision led to a number of claims based on the law of restitution (see Chapter 1). Banks claimed the right to retain money held for or recover payments from local authorities, relating to these agreements. In *Westdeutsche Landesbank Girozentrale v. Islington London Borough Council* [1996] 2 W.L.R. 802, the House of Lords confirmed that the bank was entitled to recover payments made to the local authority under the swap agreements. A bank can recover the payment even where it brings its claim outside the normal limitation period (six years) if it can establish that the payment was made under a mistake of law: *Kleinwort Benson Ltd v. Lincoln City Council* [1998] 3 W.L.R. 1095 (HL).
(2) The *ultra vires* doctrine does not apply to corporations created by Royal Charter. Nor does it any longer usually affect the contractual capacity of companies created under the Companies Act 1985.

Key Principle: **A minor is bound to pay for necessaries supplied to them.**

Nash v. Inman 1908
A Savile Row tailor supplied 11 fancy waistcoats and other items of clothing to a Cambridge undergraduate at a cost of £123.

Held: (CA) The tailor could not recover the money because the clothes were not "necessaries", as the undergraduate already had an ample supply of clothes. [1908] 2 K.B. 1

Commentary
(1) A "minor" is any person aged less than 18 years old. Until 1969 a "minor" or "infant" was any person aged less than 21 years.
(2) The Sale of Goods Act 1979, s.3 defines necessaries as goods which are suitable to the condition in life of the minor and to his actual requirements at the time of sale and delivery. Section 3 also provides that a minor need only pay a reasonable price for the necessaries, which may not be the contract price. Necessaries can include services such as education.

Key Principle: **A minor is bound by a service contract which is for their benefit.**

Chaplin v. Leslie Frewin (Publishers) Ltd 1966
A publisher agreed to publish a minor's autobiography which was to be written by journalists using information provided by the plaintiff minor and his adult wife. The plaintiffs approved the final proofs and received advance royalties from the defendants. Before publication the plaintiffs claimed that the book was libellous and inaccurate, and applied for an injunction to prevent its publication.

Held: (CA) The contract enabled the minor to become an author and so was on the whole for his benefit. An injunction would not be granted. [1966] 2 W.L.R. 40

Commentary
A minor is not bound by all beneficial contracts, only by an employment or similar contract.

Key Principle: **Where a minor agrees to buy shares in a company then the contract is voidable at the minor's option.**

Steinberg v. Scala (Leeds) Ltd 1923
A minor applied and partly paid for shares in a company. Eighteen months after the company allotted her the shares she rescinded the contract, and sued to recover the money she paid to the company.

Held: (CA) She was entitled to rescind the contract and was not liable to make any further payments for the shares. However, she was not entitled to recover the money paid because there had not been a total failure of consideration as she had been allotted the shares. [1923] 2 Ch. 452

Commentary
(1) Restitution (see Chapter 1) was the basis of her claim to recover the money paid.
(2) The company is bound by the contract. The minor is also bound, but has the option of rescinding a voidable contract during their minority or within a reasonable time of reaching the age of 18.
(3) In addition to a contract to buy shares in a company there are three other types of contract which are voidable at the minor's option: partnership agreements; contracts concerning land, *e.g.* leases; and marriage settlements.
(4) Contracts entered into by minors, other than contracts for necessaries, beneficial service contracts, and voidable contracts, are not binding on the minor, although they may be binding on the other party. See, *e.g.* the Minors' Contracts Act 1987 on the rights of the other party.

7. TERMS OF THE CONTRACT

Representations and Terms

Key Principle: **A term is not a statement which is merely an incident in preliminary negotiations; it must be understood and intended by both parties to be a term of the contract.**

Bannerman v. White 1861
D buyer was negotiating the purchase of hops from P seller. D asked P if any sulphur had been used in the treatment of the hops, adding that if it had, he would not even bother to ask the price. P said that no sulphur had been used. The negotiations led to a sale. Later D discovered that sulphur was used in five out of the 300 acres. D refused to go ahead with the contract. P sued D for the price.

Held: The statement "absence of sulphur" was a term of the contract, not a representation. (1861) 4 L.T. 740

Commentary
A representation can also be a term of the contract, *e.g.*
*Harlingdon & Leinster Enterprises Ltd v. Christopher Hull Fine Art
Ltd* (1990) (see p. 66).

Key Principle: **Where the interval between the making of the
statement and entering into the contract is well marked the
statement is likely to be a representation.**

Routledge v. McKay 1954
P and D were discussing P's purchase of D's motorcycle. On
October 23, D said, relying on the log book, that it was a 1942
model. On October 30, P and D entered into a written contract
of sale which did not refer to the date of the model. In fact it
was a 1930 model. P claimed damages for breach of contract.

Held: (CA) P could not recover damages for breach of contract. The date of the model was not a term of the contract
because of the interval between the negotiations and the contract. [1954] 1 W.L.R. 615

Commentary
(1) If, as in this case, an oral statement is not included in the
written contract, this indicates that the statement is probably not
intended to be a contractual term.
(2) Prior to the Misrepresentation Act 1967 a person in P's
position would not have been able to recover damages for
misrepresentation (see Chapter 9) unless the misrepresentation was
made fraudulently.

Key Principle: **If the person who makes the statement has
special knowledge or skill compared to the other party, then it
is more likely that the statement is a term than a
representation.**

**Dick Bentley Productions Ltd v. Harold Smith (Motors) Ltd
1965**
D, car dealers, sold a car to P, a private purchaser. D told P that
the car had only done 20,000 miles since the engine and gearbox

had been replaced. This was not correct. D was found to have been negligent. There was no apparent interval between D's statement and the contract. The contract was not reduced to writing.

Held: (CA) D was liable for breach of contract because the statement was a term of the contract. [1965] 1 W.L.R. 623

Commentary
The court distinguished this case from *Oscar Chess v. Williams* [1957] 1 W.L.R. 370, where the facts were similar except that D was a private vendor and P were car dealers. P had special skill and knowledge which they could have used to discover the age of car. In addition D was not negligent. The statement was held to be a representation not a term of the contract.

Collateral Contracts

Key Principle: **Where A gives an undertaking to B who in reliance on that statement enters into a contract with A, then the undertaking can amount to a collateral contract.**

City and Westminster Properties (1934) Ltd v. Mudd 1958
D, was a tenant of P's shop for six years. P allowed D to sleep in the shop, but did not realise that D lived in the basement. P drafted a new lease which contained a clause that in effect prohibited use of the premises other than for trade purposes. P's agent orally assured D that if he accepted the new lease D could still sleep on the premises, so D signed the lease. Subsequently P claimed forfeiture of the lease because D was still living on the premises.

Held: (ChD) D had broken a term of the lease but P's oral assurance created a collateral contract. Without that assurance D would have moved and not signed the lease. [1958] 3 W.L.R. 312

Commentary
(1) Three conditions must be satisfied for a collateral contract to come into existence:

   (a) the statement must have been intended to have contractual effect;

    (b) some indication is required that the parties intended the statement to take effect as a collateral contract rather than as a term of the main contract; and

    (c) there must be an independent offer, acceptance and consideration.

(2) See also *Shanklin Pier v. Detel Products* (1951) (see p. 42).

Express Terms

Parol Evidence Rule

Key Principle: **Neither party can bring oral evidence to add to, vary or contradict a written contract.**

Jacobs v. Batavia & General Plantations Trust 1924
P purchased $4 \times £100$ deposit notes of D's company. P relied on D's prospectus which provided for repayment of the notes in specified circumstances, in addition to the normal method of repayment. The notes did not refer to the undertaking in the prospectus. Were the contract terms just in the notes or also in the prospectus?

Held: (CA) The prospectus was a collateral contract (two judges). The third judge held that the notes and prospectus should be read together as a single contract. [1924] 2 Ch. 329

Commentary
(1) The courts have interpreted the rule less restrictively over the years.
(2) The court is not concerned with the parties actual intention but with their manifest intention, *i.e.* an objective test.

Exceptions

Key Principles: **Where a document is clearly designed to contain only part of the terms then the parol evidence rule does not apply.**

S.S. Ardennes (Cargo Owners) v. S.S. Ardennes (Owners) 1951
P were orange growers in Spain. D were shipowners. P shipped oranges to England relying on an oral promise by D that the

ship was going straight to London. In fact it went via Antwerp, so the oranges arrived late in London and P lost a favourable market. D relied on the bill of lading (written contract) which allowed them to proceed by any route.

Held: The bill of lading was not exclusive evidence of the contract. The oral promise was also part of the contract and therefore D were in breach of contract. [1951] 1 K.B. 55

Commentary
(1) This is the most important exception in practice.
(2) The practical effect of such a decision is to weaken the parol evidence rule. However, the rule remains a valuable rule of evidence, particularly in the context of conveyancing, as it provides certainty.
(3) In 1986 the Law Commission stated that the rule no longer existed.Whether a statement is a term of the contract is a question of the intention of the parties.

Interpretation of Express Terms

Key Principle: **The court should ascertain the "natural" meaning of the words, taking into account the factual background known to the parties and the "aim" of the transaction.**

Prenn v. Simmonds 1971
D claimed to be contractually entitled to acquire a 4 per cent interest in a company controlled by P, for the sum of £6,000. The interest was actually worth about £200,000. P disputed the claim on the ground that the contract provided that D could only acquire the interest if certain conditions were satisfied; in particular that the company (R.T.T.) now owned by P (who had bought it from D) should make profits of not less than £300,000 in a four-year period.

The profits of R.T.T. came to over £290,000. The profits of the R.T.T. group, *i.e.* including its subsidiary companies were more than £300,000.

Held: (HL) D was entitled to the 4 per cent interest. The reference to "profits" meant the consolidated profits of the group controlling R.T.T. and its subsidiaries. Consolidated accounts of R.T.T. and subsidiaries reflected both normal business practice and legal requirements. This interpretation would

have been an incentive for D to work for and remain with the
company; and it was linguistically accurate. [1971] 1 W.L.R. 1381

Commentary
Evidence of prior negotiations was not admitted as an aid to
interpretation.

Implied Terms

Terms Implied in Fact

Key Principle: **The court will imply a term into a particular
contract to give efficacy to the transaction.**

The Moorcock 1889
D were wharfingers who agreed to allow P shipowner to
discharge his ship at their jetty for a fee. The jetty extended into
the Thames and, as both parties realised, the ship must ground
at low water. This occurred but the ship settled onto a ridge of
hard ground below the mud, and was damaged.

Held: (CA) There was an implied undertaking by D that the
river bottom was, as far as reasonable care could provide, in
such a condition as not to endanger the ship. [1886–1890] All
E.R. Rep. 530

Commentary
(1) The court looks for the presumed intention of parties.
(2) The principle was further explained in *Shirlaw v. Southern
Foundries (1926) Ltd* [1939] 2 All E.R. 113 where MacKinnon L.J.
proposed the "officious bystander" test.
(3) The term should be *necessary* to give business efficacy to the
contract.
(4) Implied terms normally impose an obligation to take reasonable care.

Terms Implied in Law

Key Principle: **Such terms are legal incidents of particular
types of contracts, *e.g.* between employer and employee.**

Lister v. Romford Ice & Cold Storage Co. Ltd 1957
P's son was employed by D as a lorry driver. P was his mate on
the lorry. While backing his lorry, P's son drove negligently and

injured P, who sued D. D were held vicariously liable for P's negligence. D claimed an indemnity from P's son who was in breach of his contract of employment with D.

Held: (HL) The son was in breach of an implied term in his contract of employment that he would use reasonable care and skill in the performance of his duties. [1957] 2 W.L.R. 158

Key Principle: **It is an implied term in a contract of employment that an employer should take reasonable care not to injure an employee's health.**

Johnstone v. Bloomsbury Health Authority 1991
P was employed by D as a junior doctor. It was a term of the contract of employment that P should work "40 hours per week and be available for overtime of further 48 hours per week on average".

Held: (CA) D was in breach of the implied term. [1991] 2 W.L.R. 1362

Key Principle: **A landlord should take reasonable care to keep in reasonable repair and usability the common parts of a high rise block of flats.**

Liverpool City Council v. Irwin 1977
P owned a tower block. D were tenants of flats in the block . They refused to pay rent because of the poor state of the block, which was partly due to vandals and partly to D's non-cooperation. P sought an order for possession.

Held: (HL) P were not in breach of an implied obligation to keep the lifts in working order, the stairs lit, and the rubbish chutes cleared. [1977] A.C. 239

Commentary
The implied obligation must be *necessary* for the agreement to work. Lord Denning's view that the court could imply any terms it thought *reasonable* was rejected by HL.

Terms Implied by Statute

Key Principle: **A statement that a painting was by a particular artist would amount to a sale by description where the buyer relies on the statement.**

Harlingdon & Leinster Enterprises Ltd v. Christopher Hull Fine Art Ltd 1990

D sold a painting by a German expressionist artist, Gabriele Munter, to P who were dealers in German art. D had made it clear that he was not familiar with the artist's work, and that he was not an expert in regard to the painting. D's invoice described the painting as the work of Gabriel Munter. Two months later P discovered that the painting was a forgery. P sued D on the following grounds:

(i) breach of three statutory implied terms: sections 13(1), 14(2) and (3) Sale of Goods Act 1979;

(ii) misrepresentation.

At the trial the judge found for D. P appealed to CA on the section 13(1) and section 14(2) grounds.

Held: (CA) There was no breach of section 13(1) the parties could not have reasonably contemplated that P were relying on D's statement that the painting was by Gabriele Munter. Similarly there was no breach of section 14(2). The picture was of merchantable quality. It was fit for its purpose in that it could be resold or admired. [1990] 3 W.L.R. 13

Terms Implied by Custom

Key Principle: **A term can be implied by custom, so long as it is compatible with the contract.**

Hutton v. Warren 1836

A tenant was bound to farm his land in certain manner. On quitting the tenancy of his farm the tenant claimed to be entitled to fair allowance for seed and labour on the arable land.

Held: The lease should be construed in the light of this custom which was proved to exist. (1836) 1 M. & W. 466

Commentary
Trade usage can also be implied into commercial contracts, e.g. marine insurance contracts, collective agreements.

8. EXCLUSION AND LIMITATION CLAUSES

Incorporation by Signature

Key Principle: **When a document containing contractual terms is signed then in the absence of fraud or misrepresentation, the party signing it is bound.**

L'Estrange v. Graucob Ltd 1934
P bought a slot machine from D. P signed an order form which contained a clause excluding D's liability for any breach of collateral warranties. P claimed that she had not read the form and did not know what it contained.

Held: (KBD) P was bound by the clause. It was wholly immaterial whether she had read the document or not. [1934] All E.R. 16

Commentary
This principle applies to all terms not just exclusion clauses. See *Curtis v. Chemical Cleaning & Dyeing Co.* 1951 where there was misrepresentation. (p. 83).

Incorporation by Notice

Key Principle: **An exclusion clause in an unsigned document will be incorporated if the parties intend the document to have contractual force.**

Chapelton v. Barry UDC 1940
P hired a deck chair from D for three hours. P paid 2d and was given a ticket which P did not read. The ticket excluded D from liability for negligence. The deckchair collapsed as a result of D's negligence.

Held: (CA) The ticket was a mere receipt. It was not intended to have contractual force. Therefore the exclusion clause on the ticket was not incorporated into the contract. [1940] 1 All E.R. 356

Commentary
Reasonable notice of the clause is also required.

Key Principle: **An exclusion clause will be incorporated by giving reasonable notice that the document contained writing.**

Parker v. South Eastern Railway 1877
P deposited a bag in the cloakroom at D's station. P paid 2d and was given a ticket. On the front of the ticket was written "see back". On the back, there was a limitation of liability clause.

Held: (CA) Mellish L.J. said: if a person receiving a ticket:

(1) did not see or know that there was writing on the ticket, they are not bound by the clause;

(2) knew that there was writing and knew and believed that writing contained conditions then they are bound by them; and

(3) knew that there was writing on the ticket, and the delivery of the ticket to him was in such a manner as to amount to *reasonable notice* that the writing contained conditions, then he is bound by them whether or not he knew or believed that the writing contained conditions.

(1877) 2 C.P.D. 416

Key Principle: **Whether reasonable notice is given is a question of fact determined objectively.**

Thompson v. LM & S. Rly Co. 1929
P's niece purchased a railway ticket from D for P. P could not read. The ticket was issued subject to conditions which included a clause which excluded D from liability for any injury suffered by passengers. There was only one free copy of the conditions at the station. P was injured and sued D.

Held: D had taken reasonable steps to bring the conditions to public's notice. It was irrelevant that P could not read. [1929] All E.R. 474

Key Principle: **The more unusual or unexpected a particular term the higher will be the degree of notice required to incorporate it.**

Thornton v. Shoe Lane Parking Ltd 1971

P parked his car in D's car park, and when he collected it he was injured in an accident which was partly D's fault. At the entrance to the car park a notice stated: "All cars parked at owner's risk". As P drove in he took a ticket from a machine. The ticket had writing on it, including a clause which referred to conditions which were displayed inside the garage. These conditions excluded D from liability for injury to customers.

Held: (CA) P was not bound by the exclusion clause. The contract was made when the machine issued the ticket. The ticket was a mere receipt. The contract could not be altered by words on the ticket. [1971] 2 W.L.R. 585

Commentary

Lord Denning said: In any event the exclusion clause is "so wide and so destructive of rights that the court should not hold any man bound by it unless it is drawn to his attention in the most explicit way . . . In order to give sufficient notice it would need to be printed in red ink on the face of the document with a red hand pointing to it—or something equally startling."

Key Principle: **The principle of reasonable notice also applies to other types of onerous clauses.**

Interfoto Picture Library Ltd v. Stiletto Visual Programmes Ltd 1988

P hired 47 photographs to D. They were sent round in a jiffy bag with a delivery note. The delivery note contained nine conditions including a clause which provided that £5.00 per transparency per day must be paid, when they were kept more than

14 days. D did not use photos, and forgot about them. P sued D for £3,783.50.

Held: (CA) P had done nothing to draw D's attention to the particular unreasonable and extortionate condition. Therefore it was not a term of the contract. [1988] 2 W.L.R. 615

Commentary
(1) Note the similarity between this clause and a penalty clause (see p. 1) and U.T.C.C. Regs 1999.
(2) In *O'Brien v. MGN Ltd*, *The Times*, August 8, 2001, the Court of Appeal applied the judgments of Bingham L.J. and Dillon L.J. in *Interfoto* to a newspaper scratchcard game. The rules of the game provided that where there were more winners than prizes a simple draw would take place. Their Lordships held that the newspaper had fairly and reasonably brought the rules to the notice of the claimant, and that the rule was neither particularly onerous or unusual. Hale L.J. considered that the issue would make an excellent question in a contract law examination.

Key Principle: **The clause must be brought to the other party's attention before or at the time of contracting.**

Olley v. Marlborough Court 1949
An exclusion clause was in a notice in P's hotel bedroom. P's luggage was stolen.

Held: P not bound by the exclusion clause. The contract was made at the reception desk. [1949] 1 All E.R. 127

Incorporation by Course of Dealing

Key Principle: **An exclusion clause can be incorporated by a long continuous and consistent course of dealing between the two parties.**

Kendall (Henry) & Sons v. William Lillico & Sons Ltd 1968
There were three or four contracts a month for feeding-stuff between P and D over a period of three years. An oral order to

buy was placed and the seller would send a contract note soon afterwards. The note contained conditions one of which stated that the buyer would be responsible for latent defects. Young pheasants died as a result of defective feeding-stuff being supplied.

Held: (HL) The exclusion clause was incorporated in the particular transaction even though the usual steps to incorporate the clause were not taken. [1968] 2 All E.R. 444

Commentary
However, HL also held that the wording of the clause did not cover the particular breach.

Key Principle: **A term may also be implied into a contract because of a general course of dealing amounting to a trade custom or usage.**

British Crane Hire Corporation Ltd v. Ipswich Plant Hire Ltd 1975
P and D both hired out earth-moving equipment. D urgently needed a drag-line crane and orally agreed to hire one from P, who sent D a printed form for D's signature. Before D signed it the crane sank in marshy ground. The printed form contained terms whereby D would be liable to indemnify P for the loss of the crane.

Held: (CA) The indemnity clause was a term of the contract. Both parties understood that the hire would be on normal trade terms. [1974] 2 W.L.R. 856

Commentary
(1) CA distinguished Hollier v. Rambler Motors (1972) (see p. 74) where there were three or four transactions over a five-year period and where one party was a consumer.
(2) This case involves an indemnity clause, but Treitel considers that the principle is equally applicable to exclusion clauses.

Interpretation of Exclusion Clauses

Key Principle: **An exclusion clause will always be construed narrowly against the party who put it forward.**

Andrew Bros (Bournemouth) Ltd v. Singer & Co. Ltd 1933
P was appointed as dealers for "new Singer cars" by D. P contracted to buy cars under an agreement which provided inter alia that "all conditions, warranties and liabilities imposed by statute, common law or otherwise are excluded". D delivered a car which was not strictly a "new" car, as it had already been driven a considerable mileage to be shown to another customer.

Held: (CA) D could not rely on the exclusion clause, because it dealt only with *implied* terms. The obligation to deliver a new car was an *express* term. [1933] All E.R. 479

Commentary
This principle is known as the *contra proferentem* rule. See also *Morris v. C.W. Martin & Sons* (1965) at p. 49.

Key Principle: **The *contra proferentem* rule is not applied so strictly to limitation clause.**

Ailsa Craig Fishing Co. Ltd v. Malvern Fishing Co 1983
D2 agreed to provide a security service for D1's fishing boats in Aberdeen harbour. D2 were negligent and as a result D1's boat and a boat belonging to P (Malvern) sank. P sued D1 who claimed against D2. However, in the contract between D1 and D2 there was a clause which limited D2's liability to £1,000. D1's actual loss was £55,000.

Held: (HL) D2 was able to rely on the limitation clause. The clause was clear and unambiguous. It was not unlikely that a party would agree to such a clause. [1983] 1 W.L.R. 964

Commentary
(1) Lord Fraser stated that limitation clauses are not regarded "with the same hostility" as exclusion clauses. The court should consider the risks to which the defending party may be exposed,

the remuneration which he receives, and the possibility of insurance by the other party.

(2) The Court of Appeal in *BHP Petroleum Ltd v. British Steel plc* [2001] All E.R. (Comm) 133 accepted that this was the current legal position. Evans L.J. thought that it was unfortunate that a distinction between limitation and exclusion clauses was necessary. He considered that a single general rule applicable to all such clauses was preferable. This should be based on the more extreme the consequences of the clause the more stringent should be the court's approach to it.

Exclusion of Negligence Liability

Key Principle: **General words will not usually exclude liability for negligence where the party could be liable irrespective of negligence.**

White v. John Warwick & Co. Ltd 1953

P hired a bicycle from D. A clause in the agreement stated that "nothing in this agreement shall render the owners liable for any personal injuries". P was injured because of defective saddle.

Held: D was liable for negligence. The clause excluded strict liability in contract but not the tortious duty to take reasonable care. [1953] 1 W.L.R. 1285

Commentary

(1) Under U.C.T.A. 1977, s.2(1) it is no longer possible to exclude liability for negligence which causes death or personal injury. However, it is still possible to exclude liability for negligence which causes damage to property so long as the exclusion clause is reasonable (U.C.T.A. 1977, s.2(2)).

(2) The court will look at the wording of the clause to see if the intention of the party to exclude liability for negligence has been made sufficiently clear to the other party.

Key Principle: **It is advisable to use "negligence" or a synonym to exclude liability for negligence.**

Dorset County Council v. Southern Felt Roofing 1990

D, a building contractor, was engaged to repair a school belonging to P. During the work the school caught fire. The contract provided that P would "bear the risk of loss or damage in respect of . . . the existing structure . . . by fire, lightning, explosion, aircraft and other aerial devices." D argued that this was an exclusion clause.

Held: (CA) An exemption clause could exclude liability for negligence. However, by including events other than fire which might occur without human fault, the clause was intended to cover heads of liability other than negligence, and so the clause could not operate to exclude liability in negligence. [1990] 48 B.L.R. 96

Commentary
In *Shell Chemicals UK Ltd v. P & O Roadtanks Ltd* [1995] 1 Lloyd's Rep. 297, CA held that "all claims and demands whatever" was not sufficiently clear and unambiguous to cover negligence liability. In *Monarch Airlines Ltd v. London Luton Airport Ltd* [1997] C.L.C. 698 QBD held that the words "neglect or default" were wide enough to exclude such liability.

Key Principle: **General words will not always exclude liability for negligence even where the only possible liability is in negligence.**

Hollier v. Rambler Motors (AMC) Ltd 1972
D orally agreed to repair P's car. The car was damaged by a fire caused by D's negligence. On two previous occasions P had signed an invoice which contained a condition excluding D from liability for damage caused by fire to customers' cars.

Held: (CA) The wording of the clause did not exclude liability for a fire caused by D's negligence. In every case it comes down to a question of construing the exclusion clause but the wording has to be clear for negligence to be excluded. [1972] 2 W.L.R. 401

Key Principle: **Where a party to the contract has committed a particularly serious breach then the court will only permit the exclusion clause to apply where there is a clear and unambiguous intention that it should do so.**

Photo Production Ltd v. Securicor Transport Ltd 1980
D agreed to provide a night patrol service for P's factory at a weekly charge of £8.75. One of D's employees started a small fire which got out of control so that the factory, worth £650,000, was destroyed. The contract contained a clause which stated that in no circumstances would D be liable for the acts of its employees.

Held: (HL) D could rely on the exclusion clause. The words of the exclusion clause were clear. [1980] 2 W.L.R. 283

Commentary
(1) The courts will take into account:

   (a) the importance of the term broken;

   (b) the manner of the breach; and

   (c) the seriousness of the consequences of the breach.

(2) See also *Ailsa Craig Fishing Co. Ltd v. Malvern Fishing Co. Ltd* (1983) where D was able to rely on a limitation clause despite a "total" breach; and *George Mitchell (Chesterhall) Ltd v. Finney Lock Seeds* (1983).
(3) This rule of construction remains important in the context of commercial and other contracts, whose exclusion clauses are not subject to U.C.T.A.'s reasonableness test.

Unfair Contract Terms Act 1977

Meaning of "Exemption Clause"

Key Principle: **A contract term which states that a buyer cannot refuse to pay for incorrect or defective goods is an exemption clause and is subject to the Act.**

Stewart Gill Ltd v. Horatio Myer and Co. Ltd 1992
D entered into a contract with P for the supply and installation of an overhead conveyor system. D withheld the final 10 per

cent of the contract price claiming that P were in breach of contract. It was a term of the contract that "the Customer shall not be entitled to withhold payment of any amount due to the Company under the Contract by reason of any counterclaim, etc."

Held: (CA) The clause was an exclusion clause and was unreasonable under U.C.T.A., s.3. Therefore it was invalid. [1992] Q.B. 600

Commentary
(1) U.C.T.A., s.13, defines exemption clauses more widely than clauses which just exclude or limit liability.
(2) A customer who receives incorrect or defective goods is legally entitled to refuse payment for them.

Key Principle: **A clause which transfers liability in negligence from the owner to the hirer of machinery is an exclusion clause.**

Phillips Products Ltd v. Hyland 1987
P hired a JCB and a driver (D1) from D2 on standard form conditions of hire. One clause provided that drivers would be regarded as servants or agents of the hirer (P) who would alone be responsible for claims arising from the operating of plant by drivers, etc. The driver negligently damaged P's building. D2 argued that they were not vicariously liable for D1's negligence because of the clause, and that the clause transferred rather than excluded liability.

Held: (CA) The clause was an exclusion clause. It was subject to section 2(2) of U.C.T.A. It was unreasonable in relation to this particular contract because of the particular facts of the case. In particular P were not in the business of hiring; the hire was arranged at short notice; P had no opportunity to obtain insurance; and P had no say in the choice of driver. [1987] 2 All E.R. 620

Commentary
The same clause was held not to be an exclusion clause in *Thompson v. Lohan (Plant Hire) Ltd* (1987) where the claim was brought by a third party.

Key Principle: **A disclaimer which purports to exclude liability for negligent misstatement is subject to U.C.T.A. 1977.**

Smith v. Eric S. Bush 1989
P purchased a house in reliance on a valuation given by a surveyor. HL held that the surveyor was liable to P under the tort of negligent misstatement. Was a disclaimer of liability for negligence effective?

Held: (HL) The disclaimer did not prevent a duty of care arising in the first place; it excluded liability. It was subject to section 2(2) of U.C.T.A. The disclaimer was unreasonable. The court took into account that: the purchaser had no power to object to the clause; he should not be expected to obtain a second valuation; D should take responsibility for a straightforward valuation; and the decision would only have a marginal impact on insurance premiums. [1989] 2 All E.R. 514

Commentary
Liability for the tort of negligent misstatement was established in *Hedley Byrne & Co. v. Heller & Partners* [1963] 3 W.L.R. 101 (see p. 97).

"Dealing as a Consumer"

Key Principle: **Where a business enters into a contract which is incidental to its business then it is dealing as a consumer.**

R & B Custom Brokers Co Ltd v. United Dominion Trust Ltd 1988
P, a company, bought a car from D for its directors. The contract excluded liability for breach of S.G.A. 1979, s.14 (implied conditions as to fitness and quality). Under U.C.T.A., s.6 the exclusion clause was invalid if P was dealing as a consumer. The company was not in the business of car dealing. The car leaked.

Held: (CA) The car was not fit for its purpose (S.G.A. 1979, s.14(3)). The company was dealing as a consumer. The transaction was not an integral part of its business. Such a transaction would only be done in the course of business if there was a degree of regularity. [1988] 1 W.L.R. 321

Commentary
(1) "Dealing as a consumer" is relevant in deciding whether the reasonableness test referred to in U.C.T.A. 1977, sections 3, 4, 6, and 7 is applicable.
(2) The decision has been criticised because it applies however large and complex the business.

Reasonableness Test

Key Principle: The relative bargaining strength of the parties, the opportunity to purchase without an exclusion clause, and commercial practice are all factors relevant to the reasonableness of an exclusion clause.

George Mitchell (Chesterhall) Ltd v. Finney Lock Seeds Ltd 1983
D, seed merchants, agreed to supply P, a farmer, with Dutch winter cabbage seed for £192. A term of the contract purported to limit D's liability if the seed supplied was defective. D's liability was limited to replacing the seed and refunding the price. D was not liable for other loss or damage. P planted 63 acres but the seed was the wrong kind. It was unmerchantable and the crop was a total failure. P claimed £63,000 for lost production.

Held: (HL) The exclusion clause covered the loss but it was unreasonable. [1983] 2 A.C. 803

Commentary
(1) In CA Kerr L.J. listed the following factors as being relevant to reasonableness:

  (a) any fault was wholly on D's part;
  (b) P should not be expected to insure against such loss, whereas D could;
  (c) there was a grossly disproportionate and unreasonable allocation of respective risks, which was not negotiated but imposed by D;
  (d) the clause was not normally relied upon where there was a genuine and justified claim; and
  (e) the meaning and effect of the clause was obscure.

(2) Consider also *Philips v. Hyland* (1987); *Smith v. Eric S. Bush* (1989) (see p. 76).

Key Principle: **Where a clause limits liability to a specific sum of money, the sum specified should be justifiable.**

St Albans City and District Council v. International Computers Ltd 1996

D, a computer company entered into a contract on its standard terms and conditions with P, a local authority, to supply a database for the community charge register. A clause limited the company's liability for loss to £100,000. P's actual loss was £1,314,846.

Held: (CA) The clause was unreasonable under sections 3 and 11 of U.C.T.A. 1977. [1996] 4 All E.R. 481

Commentary

(1) The Court of Appeal upheld the QBD decision on reasonableness. The clause was unreasonable because:

(1) the parties were of unequal bargaining power;

(2) D could not justify the figure of £100,000; it was small considering the potential and actual loss; and

(3) D was insured £50 million worldwide; and was better able to insure against such loss than P.

(2) See also *Watford Electronics Ltd v. Sanderson CFL Ltd* [2001] 1 All E.R. (Comm) 696 where the Court of Appeal held that neither an exclusion clause nor a limitation clause in a contract for the supply of computer hardware and software was unreasonable under s.11 U.C.T.A. 1977.

Key Principle: **A limitation clause may be unreasonable where it is difficult and expensive for the other party to insure against loss.**

Salvage Association v. CAP Financial Services 1995

In 1987 P, a marine surveying company, entered into a contract with D for the design, development and supply of computer accounting software. By July 1989 the software was not complete and contained numerous errors. P sued D for breach of contract claiming approximately £850,000. D relied on clauses in the contract which limited their liability to £25,000.

Held: (QBD) D was under a contractual obligation to exercise reasonable care and so the limitation clause was subject to the reasonableness test in section 2(2). The limitation clause was unreasonable because P unlike D was effectively unable to insure, and D could not justify the limit of £25,000. [1995] F.S.R. 654

Commentary
(1) The contract came within U.C.T.A. and was not excluded from its operation by Schedule 1, para. 1(c) (creation of intellectual property rights).
(2) The contract was based on D's standard terms but P had considered and received advice on each of its standard terms, so the contract did not fall within U.C.T.A., s.3.

Unfair Terms in Consumer Contracts Regulations 1999

Key principle: **The twin requirements of good faith and significant imbalance will in practice be the factors which determine the unfairness or otherwise of a contract term.**

Director General of Fair Trading v. First National Bank plc 2001
A term in a standard form loan agreement permitted the bank to charge additional interest where a borrower defaulted on the repayment of the loan and agreed to pay off the debt by instalments over a longer period. Regulation 3(2)(b) provides that contract terms relating to the adequacy of remuneration are not subject to the fairness test.

Held: (HL) Regulation 3(2)(b) should not be interpreted broadly and did not exempt the term in question from the fairness test, because the term was concerned with the consequences of a borrower defaulting rather the adequacy of the interest charged. The term was not unfair. [2001] 3 W.L.R. 1297

Commentary
(1) Their Lordships considered that good faith implies 'open and fair dealing'.
(2) In considering 'significant imbalance' the court should look at the position of the consumer at the time they entered the contract. The obligation to pay additional interest was clearly and unambiguously expressed. There was nothing unbalanced or detrimental to the consumer in the obligation.

Exclusion Clauses and Third Parties

Key Principle: **An exclusion clause can protect a third party to the main contract where the exclusion clause creates a collateral contract.**

New Zealand Shipping v. Satterthwaite, The Eurymedon 1974 (see p. 48).

Key Principle: **A third party may be bound by an exclusion clause in a contract to which they are not party.**

Morris v. C.W. Martin & Sons Ltd 1965 (see p. 49).

9. Misrepresentation

Misrepresentation

Key Principle: **An actionable misrepresentation is a false statement of existing fact.**

Edgington v. Fitzmaurice 1885
D, a director of a company, issued a prospectus inviting loans from the public, which stated that the money would be used in the improvement of buildings and the extension of the business. This was untrue since the evidence showed that company intended to use the loans to discharge existing liabilities. P lent D money in reliance on the statement in the prospectus.

Held: (CA) The prospectus was a fraudulent misrepresentation of fact, even though it was a statement of intention. "The state of a man's mind is as much a fact as the state of his digestion" (Bowen L.J.). [1881–1885] All E.R. Rep. 59

Commentary
(1) A representation may be made by conduct as well as by words. In *Spice Girls Ltd v. Aprilia World Service BV, The Times,* April 5, 2000, the High Court held that the participation by the Spice Girls in making a film advertising motor scooters constituted a representation by conduct of the group's intention that it would not break up during the advertising contract.
(2) A false statement as to future intention is not a statement of existing fact.
(3) An actionable misrepresentation makes the contract voidable.

Key Principle: **An opinion is not usually a statement of fact.**

Bisset v. Wilkinson 1926
The vendor of land in New Zealand, which had not previously been used as a sheep farm, told a prospective purchaser that in his judgment the land could carry 2,000 sheep.

Held: (JCPC) It was an honest statement of opinion as to the capacity of the farm. It was not a representation as to its actual capacity. [1926] All E.R. 343

Key Principle: **An opinion which is either not held or could not be held by a reasonable person with the speaker's knowledge is a statement of fact.**

Smith v. Land and House Property Corp. 1884
Vendor described his property as being let to a "most desirable tenant" on certain terms "thus offering a first class investment". In fact the penultimate quarter's rent had been paid in instalments under pressure, and the previous quarter's rent had not been paid.

Held: The description "most desirable tenant" was not a mere expression of opinion, it was an untrue assertion that nothing had occurred which made the tenant undesirable. (1884) 28 Ch.D. 7

Commentary
(1) See also *BG plc v. Nelson Group Services (Maintenance) Ltd* [2002] EWCA Civ. 547.
(2) Criminal liability will also arise where a statement is a false trade description under the Trade Descriptions Act 1968.
(3) A statement of law is not a statement of fact.

Key Principle: **If a party makes a statement on some matter, it must be a full and frank statement, not partial and misleading.**

Curtis v. Chemical Cleaning & Dyeing Co 1951
D, a dry cleaner, accepted a wedding dress for cleaning. D asked P, the customer, to sign a receipt, and explained that it contained an exclusion clause which exempted him from liability for damage to beads and sequins. In fact the clause stated that the company would not be liable for "any damage howsoever arising".

Held: (CA) D's statement conveyed a false impression which amounted to a misrepresentation; so the exclusion clause was ineffective. [1951] 1 All E.R. 631

Commentary
A party to a contract is generally under no obligation to say anything. However, even saying "No" in response to a question may amount to a misrepresentation (See *e.g. Banks v. Cox*, 2000 (unreported)).

Key Principle: **If a true representation is falsified by later events, then the change in circumstances should be communicated.**

With v. O'Flanagan 1936
Negotiations took place between P and D for the sale of D's medical practice said to be worth £2,000. Four months later, a

contract of sale was entered into, by which time the practice had become worthless because of D's intervening illness.

Held: (CA) D ought to have communicated this change in circumstance to P. Therefore, the contract could be avoided. [1936] 1 All E.R. 727

Commentary
(1) The general rule is that silence does not amount to misrepresentation.
(2) Exceptions to the general rule in addition to the two cases above are:

    (a) Contracts *uberrimae fidei* (of the utmost good faith) where one party alone knows the full facts and must make full disclosure of all material facts, *e.g.* contracts of insurance.

    (b) Where there is a special relationship between parties to the contract, of a confidential or fiduciary nature, *e.g.* principal/ agent.

(3) If the parties enter into the contract under a misapprehension, then the contract may be invalidated under the doctrine of mistake (see Chapter 10).

Key Principle: **The false statement of fact must have been intended to cause and have in fact caused the representee to make the contract.**

Horsfall v. Thomas 1862
B purchased a gun with a defect. After being fired six rounds, the gun was blown to pieces. It was not clear why this happened. It appears that S, the seller, had concealed the defect. B had not examined the gun. B claimed that the contract induced by S's fraud and misrepresentation.

Held: B could not succeed because the attempt to conceal the defect had produced no effect upon his mind. (1862) 1 H. & C. 90

Key Principle: **The false statement should have affected the representee's judgment.**

Smith v. Chadwick 1884
A company prospectus contained a false statement that one Grieve was a director of the company. P bought shares relying on the prospectus, but admitted that he had never heard of "Grieve" and was, therefore, in no way influenced by the statement.

Held: (HL) P could not avoid the contract. (1884) 9 App. Cas. 187

———————

Key Principle: **The representee should have relied on the statement.**

J.E.B. Fasteners Ltd v. Marks Bloom & Co 1983
P took over a company having seen its accounts. They were inaccurate, having been negligently prepared by D. However, P had not relied on the accounts. The evidence showed that P took over the company to obtain the services of two of its directors, The state of its accounts was irrelevant.

Held: (CA) P's claim for damages was unsuccessful. [1983] 1 All E.R. 583

———————

Key Principle: **The onus is on misrepresentee to show that he was induced by the statement.**

Museprime Properties v. Adhill Properties 1990
P bought three commercial properties at an auction in reliance on representations that revised rents were yet to be agreed. On discovering that in the case of two of the properties the rents had been fixed at a level which P considered to be too low, P refused to complete the purchase because of the misrepresentation. P considered, perhaps unreasonably, that they would have been able to negotiate higher rents if the rents had still been under review.

Held: (Ch D) P could rescind because they had been induced by the representations, even if a reasonable person would not have been similarly induced. [1990] 36 E.G. 114

Key Principle: **The false statement should be the main reason for entering into the contract.**

Attwood v. Small 1838

The vendor of a mine made exaggerated and unreliable claims about its earning capacities. The buyer wanted verification of these claims and appointed experienced agents who reported that they were accurate.

Held: The buyer could not rescind the contract. He did not rely on the vendor's statements but on the report of his own agents. [1835–1842] All E.R. Rep. 258

Key Principle: **Actual and complete knowledge of the true facts will defeat the representee's claim.**

Redgrave v. Hurd 1881

P, an elderly solicitor, advertised for a younger partner who would also buy P's house. D purchased P's house in reliance on P's statements about the value of the practice. P also showed D papers concerning the value of the practice but D did not examine them. D discovered after entering into a contract to buy the house that the value of the practice was less than P claimed. P claimed specific performance of the contract.

Held: (CA) D was found to have relied on P's statement, even though D had an opportunity to examine the papers. The onus of proof was on P to show that D had *actual knowledge* of the true facts. [1881–1885] All E.R. Rep 77

Three Types of Misrepresentation

Key Principle: **A fraudulent misrepresentation is a statement made:**

(1) knowingly, or

(2) without belief in its truth, or

(3) recklessly, careless whether it be true or false.

Derry v. Peek 1889
A company, after submitting plans to a government department, obtained the passage of an Act of Parliament authorising it to run trams in Plymouth. The plans proposed the use of steam power for the trams. However, the Act as passed stated that the trams would be moved by animal power or, if the government department consented, by steam or mechanical power. The directors of the company believed that the consent would be given as a matter of course and issued a prospectus stating that the company had the right to use steam power instead of horses. P took shares in the company in reliance upon this statement. However, the government department refused its consent. The company was wound up.

Held: (HL) P's action in the tort of deceit against the directors must fail. The directors honestly believed the statement in the prospectus to be true. (1889) 14 App. Cas. 337

Commentary
(1) The claim for damages for fraudulent misrepresentation is strictly an action in the tort of deceit.
(2) The equitable remedy of rescission is also available (see p. 89).
(3) In practice fraudulent misrepresentation is rarely alleged because it is difficult to prove; and since 1967 damages have been available for negligent misrepresentation.

Key Principle: **A negligent misrepresentation is a statement made without reasonable grounds for believing it to be true.**

Howard Marine & Dredging Co. Ltd v. A. Ogden & Sons (Excavations) Ltd 1978
P quoted D a price for the hire of two sea-going barges, and told D the cubic capacity of the barges. Subsequently P told D that

the carrying capacity of each barge was about 1800 tonnes. P gave this figure because that was the weight given in Lloyd's Register. In fact the carrying capacity was correctly stated in the shipping documents as 1055 tonnes. D hired the barges. They subsequently refused to pay the hire charges when they became aware of the reduced carrying capacity and claimed damages because of P's misrepresentation.

Held: (CA) P did not have an objectively reasonable ground to disregard the figure in the ship's documents and rely on the Lloyd's Register figure. [1978] 2 W.L.R. 515

Commentary
(1) Note that, under section 2(1) of the Misrepresentation Act 1967, P had to disprove negligence rather than D prove it.
(2) Counterclaims were made by D under section 2(1) of the Misrepresentation Act 1967; the tort of negligent misstatement; and breach of collateral warranty. The second and third counterclaims were not successful.
(3) P's exclusion clause was held to be unreasonable under Misrepresentation Act 1967, section 3.

Key Principle: **An innocent misrepresentation is a false statement of existing fact which is made neither fraudulently nor negligently.**

Government of Zanzibar v. British Aerospace (Lancaster House) Ltd 2001
In 1992 Z purchased a corporate jet from BAe(LH). In 1998 Z issued a writ claiming that the contract should be rescinded because of misrepresentation or alternatively that damages should be awarded under section 2(2) or 2(1) of the Misrepresentation Act 1967. The misrepresentations alleged to have been made by BAe(LH) related to the airworthiness, reliability, design and construction of the aircraft.

Held: (QBD) Summary judgment was given in favour of BAe(LH). Rescission was no longer available as a remedy to Z because of delay. [2000] 1 W.L.R. 2333

Commentary
See below on damages for innocent misrepresentation (pp. 88–89).

Remedies for Misrepresentation

Key Principle: **A misrepresentation may become a term of the contract.**

Leaf v. International Galleries 1950
In May 1944 P purchased a painting called Salisbury Cathedral from D for £85. D represented that the artist was John Constable. Five years later P tried to sell the painting and was told that it was not painted by Constable. P brought an action for rescission of the contract to recover the purchase price.

Held: (CA) The representation was a term of the contract. P had accepted the goods and could not rescind for breach of contract. Even if P's claim was for innocent misrepresentation, P had left it too late to claim rescission. [1950] 1 All E.R. 693

Commentary
It is not clear why P did not claim damages for breach of contract.

Rescission

Key Principle: **Where a representor cannot be traced a representee can record their intention of rescinding the contract by doing some overt act that is reasonable in the circumstances.**

Car & Universal Finance Co Ltd v. Caldwell 1964
D sold and delivered a car to X in return for a cheque which bounced the next day, by which time both the car and X had disappeared. D immediately notified the police and the AA requesting them to find the car. Meanwhile X sold the car to Y car dealers who had notice of X's defective title. Y sold the car to P, who bought it in good faith.

Held: (CA) D, by asking the police and the AA to find his car, had indicated an intention to rescind the contract and from that time the title of the car reverted to D. Therefore no title to the car passed to P. [1964] 2 W.L.R. 600

Commentary
(1) Rescission does not require a court order, but note that rescission is an equitable remedy, *i.e.* available at the discretion of the court.

(2) Normally the representees should communicate their decision to rescind to the representor within a reasonable time.

Limits to the Right of Rescission

Key Principle: **Where the representee has affirmed the contract the right to rescind is lost.**

Long v. Lloyd 1958
D, a haulage contractor, advertised a lorry, which he described as being in exceptional condition. P who was also a haulage contractor noticed some defects but still purchased the lorry having been assured by D that he had told him about all its defects. Two days after the purchase P became aware of more defects. D agreed to pay half the cost of a reconstructed dynamo but denied any knowledge of a leaking oil seal. The repairs were carried out but four days later the lorry had broken down again and P asked for the return of his money.

Held: (CA) P's continued use of the defective lorry and agreeing to D's offer to share the cost of repairs amounted to affirmation of the contract. [1958] 2 All E.R. 402

Key Principle: **Where there has been a lapse of time between the making of the contract and the decision to rescind the right to rescind is lost.**

Leaf v. International Galleries 1950
(see p. 89).

Held: (CA) P should have rescinded within days of making the contract rather than after five years.

Key Principle: **Where the parties are not able to be restored to their original position the right to rescind is lost.**

Clarke v. Dickson 1858
P purchased shares in a company in reliance on a misrepresentation. The company was being wound up and P discovered the

misrepresentations and tried to rescind the contract to recover the money he paid.

Held: P could not rescind because he could not return the shares in the company now that it was being wound up. (1858) 120 E.R. 463

Key Principle: **Where a third party's rights would be affected, the right to rescind is lost.**

Phillips v. Brooks 1919
P sold a ring to X thinking that he was Sir George Bullough. X pawned the ring to D.

Held: (CA) The contract was voidable for fraud, but not void for mistake. An innocent third party (D) acquired the jewellery in good faith for valuable consideration. The contract between P and X could not be rescinded. [1918—1919] All E.R. Rep. 246

Damages

Key Principle: **In a claim for fraudulent misrepresentation the defendant is bound to make reparation for all the actual damages directly flowing from the fraudulent inducement.**

Doyle v. Olby (Ironmongers) Ltd 1969
P purchased a business from D in reliance on statements made by D during the pre-contractual negotiations. D made fraudulent representations that the business made a healthy annual profit and that two-thirds of the business was done through the shop. The implication being that P would not need to employ a salesman to visit wholesale purchasers. Despite P's best endeavours he suffered considerable losses and eventually sold the business. P was left with debts of £4,000. The trial judge assessed damages as if the representations were contractual promises and awarded P damages of £1,500.

Held: (CA) P was awarded damages of £5,500. The object of damages is to compensate P for all the loss he has suffered. Damages for fraud are assessed differently from damages for breach of contract. [1969] 2 All E.R. 119

Commentary

(1) The House of Lords in *Smith New Court Securities Ltd v. Scrimgeour Vickers (Asset Management) Ltd* 1996 3 W.L.R. 1051 approved and applied this principle. In addition Lord Browne-Wilkinson set out seven principles which should be applied by the courts when assessing damages for fraudulent misrepresentation. In particular he stated that the damage must directly flow from and have been directly caused by the transaction entered into as a result of the misrepresentation; and that the plaintiff is entitled to damages for any consequential losses.

(2) In a claim for breach of contract, the damages are normally limited to what may reasonably be supposed to have been in the contemplation of the parties.

Key Principle: **The aim of damages in the tort of deceit is to put the representee in the position they would have been in if the deceit had not been perpetrated.**

Smith Kline & French Laboratories Ltd v. Long 1989

P, pharmaceutical drug manufacturers, were induced to sell quantities of drugs by means of fraudulent misrepresentations. D paid the "ex-factory" price. P sued D for damages in the tort of deceit.

Held: (CA) P was entitled to the difference between that price and the market price. Damages were measured at the market value of the goods, not the lesser cost of replacement. [1989] 1 W.L.R. 1

Key Principle: **In a claim for negligent misrepresentation the measure of damages for negligent misrepresentation is the same as for fraudulent misrepresentation.**

Royscot Trust Ltd v. Rogerson 1991

D1 bought a car from D2. The car was bought on hire-purchase through P, a finance company. D1 and D2 represented to P that D1 had paid a 20 per cent deposit of £1,600 and so the total purchase price was £8000, when in fact D1 had paid a deposit of £1,200 and the total purchase price was £7,600. As a result P paid D2 £6,400, when it would have only been prepared to pay £4,800. D1 sold the car to X who obtained good title.

Held: (CA) P was able to recover £3,625 being the difference between the amount paid by it to D2 and the amount received from D1 before he defaulted on the payments. The measure of damages under Misrepresentation Act 1967, s.2(1) was the measure of damages for fraudulent misrepresentation. Therefore, P was able to recover from D2 any loss which flowed directly from D's misrepresentation. [1991] 3 All E.R. 294

Commentary
(1) This means unforeseeable losses are recoverable. However, on the facts the court considered that D1's act of selling the car was not unforeseeable.
(2) The judgments refer to innocent misrepresentation, but discuss the award of damages under Misrepresentation Act 1967, s.2(1) which is concerned with negligent misrepresentation.
(3) In *Smith New Court Securities Ltd v. Scrimgeour Vickers (Asset Management) Ltd* [1996] 3 W.L.R. 1051, Lords Browne-Wilkinson and Steyn implied that the decision in this case was not correct. Arguably in a claim for negligent misrepresentation damages should only be awarded for loss that is reasonably foreseeable.

Key Principle: **Damages are measured at the time the misrepresentation was discovered not at the time the contract was entered into.**

Naughton v. O'Callaghan 1990
P purchased a young racehorse at the Newmarket sales in reliance on a description of the horse's pedigree in the sales catalogue. The price paid was £31,500. Almost two years later P discovered that, because of a mix-up at the stud where the horse had been born, the horse's pedigree was not that of a thoroughbred racehorse but an American dirt track race horse. The value of the horse at the time the contract was made was about £24,500. However, its value when the misrepresentation was discovered was about £1,500. P sued D, the seller, to recover the purchase price as well as training fees and expenditure.

Held: (QBD) P recovered the damages claimed. The horse they purchased was altogether different from what they expected. It was reasonable to train and race the colt after the purchase. The horse's fall in value related to its particular circumstances not to a general fall in the market. [1990] 3 All E.R. 191

Key Principle: **The measure of damages in a claim for innocent misrepresentation is the difference between the actual value of the subject-matter at the time of the contract and the misrepresented value of the subject-matter.**

William Sindall Plc v. Cambridgeshire County Council 1994
D sold land for housing to P for £5 million. In reply to a pre-contractual enquiry as to whether D was aware of any undisclosed easements affecting the land, D had answered "not so far as the vendor is aware". In fact there were sewer pipes under the land.

Held: (CA) There was no actionable misrepresentation. If there had been, the measure of damages under section 2(2) of the Misrepresentation Act 1967 would be the difference between the actual value of the land at the time of the contract and the value of the land as represented. [1994] 1 W.L.R. 1016

Commentary
(1) Damages should not take into account the decline in market value since the contract was made. The value of the land in fact halved.
(2) Measure of damages is assessed differently under section 2(2) from section 2(1).

Key principle: **The court has the power to award damages under section 2(2) Misrepresentation Act 1967 only where the contract is subsisting and the right to rescind has not been lost.**

Government of Zanzibar v. British Aerospace (Lancaster House) Ltd 2001
Z agreed to buy a corporate jet from BA(LH). Z claimed that the contract should be rescinded or that damages should be awarded under section 2(2) Misrepresentation Act 1967 because

of misrepresentation(s) made by BA(LH) relating to the air-worthiness and reliability of the aircraft.

Held: (QBD) Rescission was no longer available as a remedy to Z. Therefore they were not entitled to damages under s.2(2). [2000] 1 W.L.R. 2333

Commentary
The court declined to follow *Thomas Witter Ltd v. T.B.P. Industries Ltd* [1996] 2 All E.R. 573 where the court held that the power to award damages under s.2(2) did not depend on a subsisting right to rescission. It only depended upon a right having existed in the past.

Exclusion Clauses and Misrepresentation

Key Principle: **A limitation on the apparent authority of an auctioneer is not an exclusion clause.**

Overbrooke Estate Ltd v. Glencombe Properties Ltd 1974
P instructed auctioneers to sell a property. The particulars of sale stated that "neither the auctioneer nor any person in the employment of the auctioneer has any authority to make or give any representation or warranty". D, who were the highest bidders at the auction alleged that three days before auction, they asked the auctioneer questions to which inaccurate answers were given which amounted to misrepresentations.

Held: (Ch D) Even if there were misrepresentations, the question was not whether the clause was reasonable under section 3 of the Misrepresentation Act 1967. Section 3 was irrelevant because the clause was a limitation on the apparent authority of auctioneers, not an exclusion clause. D knew or ought to have known that nothing told them by the auctioneer could bind P. [1974] 3 All E.R. 511

Key Principle: **The court will look behind the clause to see whether it is designed to avoid liability.**

Cremdean Properties v. Nash 1977
P purchased property from D. P then claimed rescission of the contract because of a misrepresentation about the amount of

rentable office space. In the contract of sale D disclaimed responsibility for the accuracy of the particulars of sale and stated that no misdescription would annul the contract.

Held: (CA) The disclaimer was subject to the reasonableness test if P could show that they in fact relied on the particulars of sale, and the effect of the disclaimer was to exclude D from liability. (1977) 244 E.G. 837

Key Principle: **A term in an agreement which excludes liability for representations is invalid unless reasonable.**

Lease Management Services v. Purnell Secretarial Services 1994
P leased a photocopier, making it clear that the machine supplied should be able to produce "paper plates". It did not have this feature. The lease excluded liability for representations made about the machine.

Held: (CA) The exclusion clause was unreasonable. It was overridden by representations made to P by the copier salesman. [1994] C.C.L.R. 127

Commentary
The reasonableness test is to be found in section 3 Misrepresentation Act 1967 as substituted by section 8 Unfair Contract Terms Act 1977. See also *Curtis v. Chemical Cleaning & Dyeing Co.* (1951), and *Howard Marine & Dredging Co. Ltd v. A. Ogden & Sons (Excavations) Ltd* (1978).

Negligent Misstatement

Key Principle: **Precontractual statements made negligently can give rise to liability in the tort of negligent misstatement.**

Esso Petroleum Co Ltd v. Mardon 1976
P made statements to D, during pre-contractual negotiations, estimating the likely quantity of petrol a filling station would sell over a three-year period. The estimates were over optimistic

and D lost money. P sued for possession of the site and D claimed damages for the false representations.

Held: (CA) P recovered damages under the tort of negligent misstatement. P owed D a duty of care. P had a financial interest in the advice they were giving and knew that D was relying on their knowledge and expertise. P were in breach of the duty of care. [1976] 2 W.L.R. 583

Commentary
(1) CA also held that Esso had given a contractual warranty that their opinion was carefully formed.
(2) The facts arose before the Misrepresentation Act 1967 became law. Therefore, D could not claim under section 2(1).
(3) The tort of negligent misstatement derives from the decision of the House of Lords in *Hedley Byrne & Co v. Heller & Partners* [1963] 3 W.L.R. 101.

10. MISTAKE

Key Principle: **The mistake must occur at the time of making the contract.**

Amalgamated Investment and Property Co. Ltd v. John Walker & Sons Ltd 1976
P was negotiating to buy a warehouse from D. D knew that P intended to redevelop the property. Both P and D knew that P required planning permission to do so. P asked D if the property was of special historical or architectural interest. On August 14, D truthfully replied that it was not. Unknown to P and D, the Department of Environment planned to make the warehouse a listed building. On September 26, P entered into a contract to buy the property for £1.71 million. On September 27, the Department of Environment made it a listed building, and it became worth £210,000.

Held: (CA) P could not rescind for common mistake. The parties were not mistaken about the nature of the building at the date of the contract. [1976] 3 All E.R. 509

Common Mistake

Key Principle: **Where unknown to both parties the specific subject matter of the agreement is in fact non-existent then the contract is void for common mistake.**

Couturier v. Hastie 1856
There was a contract for the sale of a cargo of corn thought to be in transit from Salonika to the U.K. Unknown to both parties the corn had fermented and was sold by the master of the ship in Tunis.

Held: (HL) It was a contract to buy specific goods, which in fact did not exist. The buyer did not have to pay for the corn. The contract was in effect void. [1843–1860] All E.R. Rep. 280

Commentary
(1) This is known as *res extincta.*
(2) Both parties make the same mistake.
(3) Sale of Goods Act 1979 states that a contract for sale of specific goods which have perished is void. (section 6)
(4) In *McRae v. Commonwealth Disposals Commission* (1951) the High Court of Australia adopted a different approach. The court awarded damages for breach of an implied term that the subject matter of the contract existed. A similar approach was adopted in *Associated Japanese Bank (International Ltd) v. Credit du Nord* [1988] 3 All E.R. 902.

Key Principle: **Where A agrees to buy property from B, which both A and B believe is owned by B, but which in fact belongs to A, then the contract if void for common mistake.**

Cooper v. Phibbs 1867
A man erroneously believed that he owned a fishery, and told his nephew that he did. After his uncle's death his nephew leased the fishery from his uncle's daughters. In fact the nephew owned the fishery.

Held: (HL) The contract was set aside, but the daughters were given a lien on the fishery for such money as they had spent on it. (1867) L.R. 2 HL 149

Commentary
(1) This is known as *res sua*.
(2) Both parties made the same mistake.

Key Principle: **Where both parties enter into a contract under a false and fundamental assumption then as a general rule the contract is valid.**

Bell v. Lever Brothers 1932
P, Lever Brothers, made D, the managing director of a subsidiary company, redundant. P agreed to pay D £30,000 compensation. After paying D the money P discovered that they could have dismissed D for breach of his duties as a director. Therefore P sued D for the return of the £30,000 on the basis of common mistake.

Held: (HL) The fundamental assumption that the contract was not terminable turned out to be false but this did not affect the validity of the contract. [1932] A.C. 161

Commentary
(1) The effect of this decision is that the only false assumption which will amount to an operative mistake is that which relates to the very existence of subject matter of the contract. However, in *Grains & Fourrages S.A. v. Huyton* [1997] 1 Lloyd's Rep. 628 an agreement was held not to be binding because it was based on both parties' common and fundamental mistake concerning the tonnage of the goods. Compare *Rose v. Pim* [1953] (see below).
(2) The type of common mistake in this case is sometimes referred to as "mistake as to quality".

Key Principle: **Where the contract is not void for common mistake the court may still exercise its equitable jurisdiction to set aside the contract.**

Solle v. Butcher 1949
In 1947 D let a flat to P for seven years at an annual rent of £250. The flat had been let in 1938 at £140. Both P and D thought that the flat was no longer subject to the rent restriction legislation

because of improvements and alterations. Two years later P sued D claiming that the flat was subject to the rent restriction legislation and so the rent should have been £140. D sought to have the lease set aside on the ground of mistake.

Held: (CA) There was a common mistake. The rent of the flat was subject to the rent legislation, but the contract was not void. However, using its equitable jurisdiction the court set aside the lease and gave P the option of either a new lease being granted on similar terms but allowing for an increased statutory rent, or surrendering the lease. [1949] 2 All E.R. 1107

Commentary
In *Nutt and Another v. Read and Another* (1999), *The Times*, December 3, 1999, the Court of Appeal held that a tenancy of a chalet granted on the basis of a common mistake was voidable, and could be rescinded.

Key Principle: **Common mistake does not make the contract void where the parties appear to be in full and certain agreement.**

Rose v. Pim 1953
P asked D to supply them with "feveroles". D told P that feveroles were just horsebeans, and supplied horsebeans. In fact feveroles were a different kind of bean. P sought rectification of the contract.

Held: (CA) The contract was not void for mistake. P had delayed too long in making the application for rectification of the contract. [1953] 2 All E.R. 739

Commentary
Rectification would have meant replacing "horsebeans" with "feveroles".

Key Principle: **Where the contract is not void for mistake the court may still exercise its equitable jurisdiction to rectify the written agreement.**

Joscelyne v. Nissen 1970
P, the father, sued D, his daughter, for breach of a written contract whereby he agreed to transfer his business to D in return for being allowed to occupy his flat in his daughter's house free from rent and other outgoings. D paid the gas, electricity and coal bills until a dispute arose between the parties.

Held: (CA) The court ordered rectification of the contract so that these items were specifically mentioned, because there was convincing proof that the written contract did not represent the parties common intention. [1970] 1 All E.R. 1213.

Mutual Mistake

Key Principle: **Where there is no genuine agreement between the parties because they are at cross-purposes, there is no binding contract.**

Scriven Bros & Co v. Hindley 1913
P sold goods at auction to D. P was selling both hemp and tow in two lots, but they were not clearly distinguished. D thought both lots were hemp which was more expensive than tow. So D paid a much higher price for the tow than was necessary. Therefore P intended to sell tow, but D intended to buy hemp.

Held: (KBD) There was no binding contract because there was no certainty as to what was the subject matter of the contract. [1913] 3 K.B. 564

Commentary
Note the overlap with contract formation.

Key Principle: **Where there is a mutual mistake which does not invalidate the contract, an equitable remedy may be available.**

Denny v. Hancock 1870

D purchased a house and grounds. Before entering into the contract to buy the property he had inspected the property with a plan and believed that three magnificent trees were within the boundaries. He then discovered that they were not. D refused to proceed with the purchase and P sued for specific performance.

Held: There was a binding contract. However, the court declined to make a decree of specific performance because the plan was confusing and the physical boundary was misleading when physically inspected. (1870) L.R. 6 Ch. App. 1

Unilateral Mistake

Key Principle: **Where P could not have reasonably supposed that the offer reflected D's real intention the contract is void for mistake.**

Hartog v. Colin & Shields 1939

D offered to sell hareskins to P at 10¼d per pound. Preliminary negotiations with P had taken place on the basis of 10¼d per piece. In the hareskin trade skins were always sold per piece. There were about three pieces to the pound so D's offer amounted to 3¼d per piece, whereas three weeks earlier the price had been 10¼d per piece.

Held: (QBD) P must have realised D's mistake, therefore the contract was void. [1939] 3 All E.R. 566

Commentary

(1) Most cases involving unilateral mistakes arise because of mistaken identity usually involving a "rogue".

(2) In order to make the contract void the mistake as to identity must be fundamental.

(3) The onus is on the person deceived to rebut the presumption that there is valid contract.

Key Principle: **At the time of negotiating the contract, the identity of the other party must be of crucial importance to the mistaken party and this must be apparent from their conduct during the negotiations.**

Cundy v. Lindsay 1878

A rogue, "Blenkarn", writing from 37 Wood Street, Cheapside, offered to buy goods from P. The rogue signed his letters so that the signature looked like "Blenkiron & Co", which was a respectable firm at 123 Wood Street, Cheapside. The rogue intended to mislead because his address was a single room, and the street entrance was in an adjoining street. P knew of Blenkiron and without checking sent goods to Blenkiron, 37 Wood Street. The rogue sold them to D who took them in good faith. P sued D for conversion.

Held: (HL) P intend to sell to Blenkiron not to the person who traded at 37 Wood Street. Therefore, the contract was void for unilateral mistake, and P could recover the goods from D. [1878] 3 App. Cas. 459

Commentary

See *Citibank N.A. v. Brown Shipley & Co. Ltd* [1991] 2 All E.R. 690 where the court held that the identity of a messenger, to whom P handed over a banker's draft in favour of D, was not of fundamental importance. The draft was valid.

Key Principle: **The mistaken party must prove that he intended to deal with some person other than the person with whom he apparently made the contract.**

King's Norton Metal Co. Ltd v. Edridge Merrett & Co. Ltd 1897

Wallis, with deception in mind, set up in business as Hallam & Co. Using impressive headed notepaper, he ordered goods on credit from P, which W then sold to D. There had been previous dealings between W & P. W did not pay for the goods. P tried to recover the value of goods from D on the grounds that the contract between P and W was void, since P mistakenly believed that such a firm as Hallam & Co. existed. Therefore, the title to the goods still remained with them.

Held: (CA) P was unsuccessful. P intended to contract with the writer of the letter. P was unable to show that they meant to contract with Hallam & Co. rather than with W. [1897] 14 T.L.R 98

Commentary
The contract was voidable for fraud, but because it had not been avoided at the time of the sale by W to D, D had good title to the goods.

Key Principle: **Where a rogue is not the hirer named in a written hire purchase agreement, the rogue cannot be a "debtor" under that agreement.**

Shogun Finance Ltd v. Hudson 2001

A rogue claiming to be "Mr Patel" wanted to buy a new car from a car dealer on hire purchase. The rogue produced a genuine driving licence as evidence of his name and address. The dealer telephoned the claimant finance company which in a few minutes checked "Mr Patel's" identity and creditworthiness, as well as comparing faxed copies of the rogue's signature with the signature on the driving licence. The claimant told the dealer that the finance was available to "Mr Patel", and the dealer on receipt of a 10 per cent deposit handed over the car and its documentation to the rogue. The rogue sold the car to D who bought the car as a private purchaser in good faith. The claimant sought to recover the car from D.

Held: (CA) Dyson L.J., with whom Brooke L.J. agreed, held that the rogue was not "the debtor" under the written hire purchase agreement because he was not in fact "Mr Patel" and therefore D could not rely on section 27 of the Hire Purchase Act 1964, as amended. As a consequence D's contract with P was void, D had not acquired title to the car, and either had to return the car or its value to the claimants. [2001] All E.R. (D) 306

Commentary
(1) The Hire Purchase Act 1964, s.27, as amended, provides that a private purchaser who buys an article in good faith from someone who turns out only to have it on hire purchase obtains a good title.

(2) Dyson L.J. also considered that the dealer was not acting as an agent for the claimant finance company, and so the contract between the rogue and the claimant was not made "face-to-face". The identity of the hirer was of the greatest importance to the claimant which intended to hire the vehicle to "Mr Patel".
(3) Sedley L.J. (dissenting) considered that the claimant had no good reason for believing that the rogue was who he said he was, and should bear the loss.
(4) In March 2002 D applied for leave to appeal to the House of Lords.

Key Principle: **The mistaken party must prove that the other party was aware of the mistake.**

Hardman v. Booth 1863
P called at the place of business of Gandell & Co. and were fraudulently persuaded by a clerk, Edward Gandell, that he had authority to act for the firm. P sold and delivered goods to Gandell & Co., but they were intercepted by EG who pledged the goods to D. P sued D in the tort of conversion.

Held: P could recover the goods from D. No contract came into existence because P's offer was to the company, as EG knew, but EG tried to accept the offer for himself. EG, therefore, acquired no title to the goods which he could transfer to the innocent D. [1863] 1 H. & C. 803

Key Principle: **In a face to face transaction, the mistaken party must take reasonable steps to verify the identity of the person with whom they are dealing.**

Lewis v. Averay 1972
A rogue, pretending to be the actor Richard Greene (Robin Hood), offered to buy P's car and did so with a worthless cheque. P saw Richard Greene's identity pass for Pinewood Studios. P handed over the car to the rogue who sold it to D. P sued D for conversion.

Held: (CA) P had concluded a contract with the rogue. P intended to sell to the person in front of him. P had done little to verify the rogue's identity. [1973] 1 W.L.R. 510

Commentary
(1) There are two earlier CA decisions on this point. *Phillips v. Brooks Ltd* (1919) [1918–1919] All E.R. Rep. 246 (see p. 91) was followed; the court expressed disagreement with the decision in *Ingram v. Little* [1960] 3 W.L.R. 504.
(2) In *Shogun Finance Ltd v. Hudson 2001* (see above) Sedley L.J. (dissenting) considered that the claimant, using the dealer as its agent, had in law contracted "face-to-face" with the rogue. His view was that the circumstances were insufficient to rebut the presumption that the contract was with the rogue rather than the person he claimed to be. This meant that the rogue was the 'debtor' and that D was entitled to rely upon section 27 HPA 1964 and keep the car.
(3) Brooke and Sedley L.JJ. considered that the law relating to who should bear the loss in these circumstances was in an unsatisfactory state and should be reformed.

––––––––––

Key Principle: **Where a contract is not void for unilateral mistake, the court exercising its equitable jurisdiction may still provide additional remedies.**

Thomas Bates and Son v. Wyndhams (Lingerie) Ltd 1981
P, landlords, sought rectification of a lease. D had been tenants of P under two previous leases, which gave D an option to renew the lease and provided for arbitration in the event of P and D being unable to agree the new rent. The third lease by an oversight did not include a provision for fixing the rent by arbitration if the parties could not agree.

Held: (CA) P could obtain rectification. P could show that they thought the lease contained such a term; D was aware of the omission and knew that it was a mistake on P's part; D did not draw the mistake to P's attention; the mistake benefited D. [1981] 1 All E.R. 1077

Non est factum

Key Principle: **Where A is induced by the false statement of B to sign a written document containing a contract that is fundamentally different in character from that which A contemplated, then A is not bound by the contract.**

Saunders v. Anglia Building Society 1970
P, a widow aged 78, gave the deeds of her house to her nephew so that he could raise money using the house as security. P made it a condition that she could stay in the house until she died. A document was prepared which assigned the leasehold not by way of gift to the nephew, but by way of sale to the dishonest D. P signed the document. She did not read it because she had broken her glasses, and her nephew told her that it was a deed of gift to him. D, who paid no money to P or to her nephew, mortgaged the house to the building society, but failed to pay any mortgage instalments. P sued D and the building society, pleading *non est factum* on the ground that she intended to *give* the house not *sell* it.

Held: (HL) This distinction was not fundamental. The assignment was not totally different in character and nature from what she had in mind. Its object was to enable her nephew to raise a loan. [1970] 3 W.L.R. 1078

Commentary
(1) HL considered that plea of *non est factum* is not limited to deeds. It is applicable to other documents.
(2) There is a heavy burden of proof on the person raising the plea.

Key Principle: **The plea of *non est factum* applies where without negligence a person fails to scrutinise a document which they have signed.**

Lloyds Bank v. Waterhouse 1990
D was illiterate and signed a bank guarantee without reading it or telling the bank that he could not read, but in reliance on the bank's misrepresentations about its nature.

Held: (CA) D was entitled to rely on defence of *non est factum*, as well as on the bank's negligent misrepresentation. *The Independent*, February 27, 1990

11. UNFAIR PRESSURE

Duress

Key Principle: **At common law, actual violence or threats of violence to the person to pressurise that person into entering into a contract make the contract voidable and possibly void.**

Barton v. Armstrong 1975
P, was the managing director of a company. He arranged that the company would pay money to D, the chairman of the company, in order to get him off the board. P did this partly for commercial reasons, and partly because D had threatened to have P killed if P did not make the arrangement. P applied to the court to have the contract set aside for duress.

Held: (JCPC) P might have entered into the arrangement even if there had been no threats or unlawful pressure from D, but the threats and unlawful pressure contributed to his decision to enter into the arrangement. Once the fact of duress was established the burden was on D to show that the duress did not in fact induce the contract. [1975] 2 All E.R. 465

Undue Influence

Actual Undue Influence

Key Principle: **Where a contract is induced by improper pressure, not amounting to duress, it is voidable.**

Williams v. Bayley 1866
P's son had given D promissory notes on which he had forged his father's signature. P was threatened with the criminal prosecution of his son and so agreed to make an equitable mortgage in favour of D in exchange for the return of the promissory notes.

Held: (HL) The agreement could be cancelled. P did not make a free and voluntary decision. (1866) L.R. 1 HL 200

Key Principle: **Where actual undue influence is proved it is not necessary to establish manifest disadvantage.**

CIBC Mortgages Plc v. Pitt 1993
Mr Pitt persuaded his wife, D, to mortgage the jointly owned family home in order to discharge the existing mortgage and to buy a holiday home. The mortgage was obtained from P, who applied for possession of the house when the mortgage payments were not made.

Held: (HL) Where a wife was induced by the undue influence of her husband to charge the matrimonial home as security for a loan made to them jointly, the lender would not be affected by the undue influence if the husband was not his agent and if the lender had no actual knowledge of the undue influence, nor was there any indication that the transaction was anything other than a normal loan to a married couple for their joint benefit. [1993] 4 All E.R. 433.

Commentary
(1) D was able to set aside the agreement she made with her husband because of his actual undue influence. However, she was not able to set aside the mortgage as against P.
(2) See also *UCB Corporate Services Ltd v. Williams, The Times,* May 27, 2002.

Presumed Undue Influence

Where a Special Relationship Exists Between the Parties

Key Principle: **Where a special relationship exists between the parties there is a presumption that one party acted under a pressure which they could not resist.**

Allcard v. Skinner 1887
P, a woman aged 35, was introduced by her spiritual adviser, X, to D, who was the Lady Superior of the "Sisters of the Poor". X was their spiritual director and confessor. Three years later P became a sister. She took a vow of poverty which required her to surrender absolutely and forever all of her property. P remained a sister for eight years. During that period she gave £7,000 to the sisterhood. By the time she left £1,671 had been

spent. 6 years after P left she sought to recover the £1,671 on the grounds of undue influence.

Held: (CA) P could not recover the money because she did not claim immediately after leaving the sisterhood. There was undue influence. Although no personal pressure was placed on P, and no unfair advantage taken of her, the gifts were made under a pressure she could not resist. [1886–1890] All E.R. Rep. 90

Presumed Undue Influence

Where no Special Relationship Exists Between the Contracting Parties

Key Principle: **The burden of proving that undue influence has been exercised normally lies on the party challenging the validity of the agreement.**

Lloyds Bank v. Bundy 1974

D was an elderly farmer, whose home and only asset was a farm house. D, his son, and the son's company all banked at the same branch of P's bank. The son's company ran into financial difficulties. D guaranteed his son's overdraft with a charge on the farm house together with a subsequent guarantee and charge. In total the amount charged against the house was £7,500. The house was worth £10,000. D was advised by his solicitor that he should not commit himself further, but P's assistant manager arranged for another charge which would increase the total to £11,000. He told D that this was the only way P could support his son's company. In May 1970 receivers were appointed to the company and P attempted to enforce the guarantee and charges.

Held: (CA) The guarantee and charges were set aside. D looked to P for financial advice and placed confidence in it. It was in P's interest to obtain the guarantee. P should have ensured that D received independent advice. [1974] 3 All E.R. 757

Key Principle: **The presumption will be raised where a transaction is large or improvident and the person giving effect to the transaction places great trust and confidence in the recipient.**

Goldsworthy v. Brickell 1987
P, aged 85, let his farm at a very low rent to D, with a favourable option to purchase. D was a neighbouring farmer whom P came to trust and depend on for advice and help in running the farm.

Held: (CA) The agreement was set aside. Their relationship raised a presumption of undue influence. P had not entered the agreement after full, free and informed thought. [1987] 2 W.L.R. 133

Commentary
(1) In *Royal Bank of Scotland plc v. Etridge (No. 2)* [2001] 3 W.L.R. 1021 (see facts below), Lord Nicholls confirmed that there are two elements to establishing presumed undue influence: (1) the complainant placed trust and confidence in the other party; and (2) the transaction is not readily explicable by the relationship of the parties.
(2) Lord Nicholls stated that undue influence means that influence has been misused. Reasonable or even exaggerated statements by a husband would not usually amount to undue influence or misstatements. Inaccurate explanations or decisions taken by a husband on his wife's behalf which are in his interest rather than hers are likely to amount to an abuse of his influence.
(3) Where both elements are established the law reverses the burden of proof and requires the other party to provide an explanation for the transaction which may or may not rebut the presumption of undue influence.

Key principle: **The transaction is explicable only on the basis that advantage has been taken of the complainant**

Royal Bank of Scotland plc v. Etridge (No. 2) 2001
(See facts below)

Held: (HL) Lord Nicholls stated that the label 'manifest disadvantage' which had been used for the second element of presumed undue influence was ambiguous in the context of wives guaranteeing payment of their husband's business debts, and should be discarded. He preferred Lord Scarman's more detailed formulation in *National Westminster Bank plc v. Morgan* [1985] A.C. 686, and considered that the greater the disadvantage to the vulnerable person the more cogent must be the explanation before the presumption can be rebutted. [2001] 3 W.L.R. 1021

Commentary
(1) Lord Nicholls considered that the label 'manifest disadvantage' may still be apt when applied to straightforward transactions such as a substantial gift or a sale at an undervalue.
(2) Lord Scott argued that it is the combination of relationship and the nature of the transaction that gives rise to the presumption.

Equitable Remedy of Rescission

Key Principle: **The court can set aside the contract in such a way that justice can be achieved in the particular case.**

O'Sullivan v. Management Agency and Music Ltd 1984
P, Gilbert O'Sullivan, was an young unknown composer and performer when he entered into a management agreement with D. P had no business experience and completely trusted D. As a consequence P entered into various agreements put forward by D without any independent advice. D also had a financial interest in the agreements.

Held: (CA) D was in a fiduciary relationship with P, and the agreement could be set aside because of the undue influence, even though *restitutio in integrum* was not strictly possible. D was entitled to be paid for the work he had undertaken on P's behalf. [1984] 3 W.L.R. 448

Commentary
This case is also relevant to contracts in restraint of trade (see p. 135).

Key Principle: **The aim of the court is to achieve practical justice for both parties.**

Cheese v. Thomas 1994

There was an agreement between P and D, his great-nephew. P gave D £43,000 which was to be put towards the cost of a house for them both. D bought the house in his sole name for £83,000. P had the right to live in the house for the rest of his life. D defaulted on the mortgage. The house was sold for £55,400. It was accepted that P had entered into the transaction as a result of D's undue influence. P claimed £43,000.

Held: (CA) P could only recover the same proportion of the selling price of £55,400 as he had contributed towards the purchase (*i.e.* just over half). [1994] 1 W.L.R. 129

Commentary

(1) The payment was accepted to be for purchase of property in which P would have rights rather than a loan.
(2) The equitable remedy of rescission aims to restore both parties to their original position.

Key Principle: **The wife's right to set aside the transaction is an "all or nothing" process.**

TSB Bank plc v. Camfield 1995

The bank had constructive notice of a misrepresentation by H which had induced W to charge the matrimonial home so that a loan could be made to his business. H had innocently misrepresented that the loan was limited to £15,000 when in fact it was unlimited. P claimed they could recover £15,000.

Held: (CA) W could have the whole transaction set aside. Terms should not be imposed on W as a condition of her obtaining equitable relief. In any event W had nothing to return to the bank as she had received nothing from the bank. [1995] 1 All E.R. 951

Commentary

However, in *Barclays Bank plc v. Caplan, The Times,* December 12, 1997, the court (Ch D) held that setting aside was not invariably an all or nothing process. The court could not rewrite an agreement, but where one (or more) part of a document was tainted by undue influence it could be severed and set aside leaving the remainder of the agreement valid.

Third Party Rights

Key Principle: **A creditor will have constructive notice of undue influence where a wife offers to stand surety for her husband's debt, the transaction is not to her financial advantage and there is a substantial chance that the husband has committed a legal or equitable wrong in procuring his wife's agreement.**

Barclays Bank Plc v. O'Brien 1993

H and W jointly owned their matrimonial home. H's company had an overdraft. P required security for the overdraft from H. This included a mortgage on the matrimonial home which had to be agreed to and signed by W. W signed the mortgage and an accompanying explanatory letter at the bank in the presence of H. H had told W that the mortgage was for £60,000 and would last three weeks when in fact it was unlimited on both counts. P sought possession of the matrimonial home. W claimed that she was induced to sign the mortgage as a result of H's undue influence and misrepresentations. The undue influence claim was rejected by the trial judge. The hearing in HL was on the misrepresentation and constructive notice points.

Held: (HL) P was fixed with constructive notice of the wrongful misrepresentations made by H to W who was therefore entitled as against P, to have the mortgage set aside. [1993] 4 All E.R. 417

Commentary

(1) Lord Browne-Wilkinson stated that the same principles are applicable to any case where there is an emotional relationship between the cohabitees, whether heterosexual or homosexual, or any other relationship based on trust and confidence, and the bank is aware of the relationship.

(2) In *Royal Bank of Scotland plc v. Etridge (No. 2)* [2001] 3 W.L.R. 1021 Lord Nicholls preferred the phrase 'put on inquiry' to 'constructive notice'. He considered that a bank is put on inquiry whenever a wife offers to stand surety for her husband's

debts, or for the debts of a company whose shares are held by her and her husband. Where money is advanced to a husband and wife jointly, the bank is not put on inquiry unless the bank is aware that the loan is being made for the husband's purposes as distinct from their joint purposes (see *CIBC Mortgages plc v. Pitt* 1994, above). (3) Lord Nicholls also considered that the key principle (above) constituted the underlying rationale but did not amount to factual conditions that must be proved in each case before a bank is put on inquiry.

Key Principle: **A creditor may have constructive notice of undue influence exercised over an employee by an employer.**

Credit Lyonnais Bank Nederland N.V. v. Burch 1997

D, an employee, agreed to her employer's request to put up her flat as security for a £20,000 extension to his company's overdraft. P advised D in writing to obtain independent legal advice, which she declined to do. In fact D provided P with an unlimited guarantee of her employer's debts.

Held: (CA) The mortgage and guarantee were set aside. The transaction was so manifestly to D's disadvantage that the bank could not claim to have taken reasonable steps to avoid being fixed with constructive notice of the employer's undue influence. [1997] 1 All E.R. 144

Commentary

In *Royal Bank of Scotland plc v. Etridge (No. 2)* [2001] 3 W.L.R. 1021, Lord Nicholls confirmed that the *O'Brien* principle was of wider application. He stated that as a general principle banks should be "put on inquiry" in every case where the relationship between the surety and the debtor is non-commercial, as in *Burch* or, for example, where there is a parent-child relationship.

Key Principle: **The bank should be expected to take reasonable steps to satisfy itself that the wife understood the nature and effect of the transaction she was entering into.**

Royal Bank of Scotland plc v. Etridge (No. 2) 2001

The House of Lords heard eight appeals together. In each case a wife had agreed to the matrimonial home being used as security for a loan by a bank to her husband or to her husband's company. Subsequently in seven of the cases the bank sought possession of the matrimonial home because the loan was not repaid. Each wife resisted the bank's application on the ground that her agreement had been obtained by her husband's undue influence (and that she had not received independent legal advice before agreeing to the matrimonial home being used as security for the loan—see below).

Held: (HL) (see below). [2001] 3 W.L.R. 1021

Commentary
(1) Lord Nicholls set out what amounted to reasonable steps. He stated that in future a bank should (1) check directly with the wife the name of the solicitor she wishes to act for her, and (2) should inform W that it requires written confirmation from the solicitor that W has been independently advised of the legal and practical implications of the proposed transaction.
(2) Lord Scott stressed that the bank is not required to satisfy itself that there has been no undue influence, unless it is aware of facts from which undue influence can be presumed.
(3) The bank should not proceed with the transaction until it has received from W the name of her solicitor.
(4) The solicitor acting for W may also act for the bank or for H, unless there is evidence of undue influence or other impropriety by H.

Nature and Extent of Independent Legal Advice

Key Principle: **The wife's solicitor is under a duty to satisfy him/herself that his/her client understands the nature and effect of the transaction and is willing to enter into it.**

Royal Bank of Scotland plc v. Etridge (No. 2), Barclays Bank plc v. Harris, Midland Bank plc v. Wallace, National Westminster Bank plc v. Gill, UCB Home Loans Corporation Ltd v. Moore, Barclays Bank plc v. Coleman, Bank of Scotland v. Bennett, Kenyon-Brown v. Desmond Banks & Co 2001
The House of Lords heard these eight appeals together. In each case a wife had agreed to the matrimonial home being used as security for a loan by a bank to her husband or to her husband's company. Subsequently in seven of the cases the bank sought

possession of the matrimonial home because the loan was not repaid. Each wife resisted the bank's application on the ground that she had not received independent legal advice before agreeing to the matrimonial home being used as security for the loan (and that her agreement had been obtained by her husband's undue influence). In three of the seven cases the court had rejected the wife's defence at a preliminary stage. In the other four cases the wife had been unsuccessful at the trial. The eighth case concerned a claim by a wife for damages from a solicitor who advised her before she entered into the transaction.

Held: (HL) The appeals in three cases (*Harris, Wallace, Moore*) were allowed on the ground that the wife had an arguable defence that the bank had not taken reasonable steps to satisfy itself that the wife had received independent legal advice as to the nature and effect of the transaction she entered into. The appeal by the wife in *Bennett*, one of the four cases that went to trial, was successful as was the appeal by the solicitor in the eighth case (*Kenyon-Brown*). The appeals in the other three cases (*Etridge, Gill, Coleman*) were dismissed, either because the wife failed to establish at trial that she had been subject to undue influence, or because constructive notice of undue influence could not be imputed to the bank. [2001] 3 W.L.R. 1021

Commentary
(1) The aim is to ensure that W receives true independent advice from her solicitor as to the nature and effect of the transaction so that she is able to give genuine consent. The solicitor is not under a duty to satisfy him/herself of the absence of undue influence.
(2) The wife's solicitor is under a duty is to explain to W (1) the legal and practical effect of the transaction, (2) that W has the choice whether or not to proceed, and (3) that the solicitor is required to confirm to the bank that W has been so advised
(3) The House of Lords disagreed with the Court of Appeal's formulation of a solicitor's duty in such cases. An informed wife is not to be stopped from entering into a financially unwise transaction should she wish to do so, and she should not be able to subsequently plead that the bank had constructive notice of any undue influence.
(4) The bank should provide the solicitor with detailed financial and other relevant information so that the solicitor can ensure that

W appreciates the seriousness of the risks she is taking, and can identify any reasons why the transaction may not be in her best interests.

(5) The solicitor's discussion with W should take place at a face to face meeting in the absence of H.

(6) Normally a bank should be able to rely upon the written confirmation from W's solicitor that she has been properly advised, unless the bank has reason to suspect that such advice has not been given.

(7) Where the solicitor wrongly advises W or wrongly confirms to the bank that she has received independent advice, W's remedy will be against the solicitor.

Economic Duress

Key Principle: **Economic duress renders a contract voidable.**

Pao On v. Lau Yiu Long 1979

P threatened to break a contract with X company unless D who were shareholders in the company gave P a guarantee against loss resulting from the performance of that contract. D thinking that the risk of such loss was small, gave the guarantee to avoid the adverse publicity which the company might suffer if the contract was not performed.

Held: (JCPC) In the circumstances there was no coercion of the will so the guarantee was not vitiated by duress. [1980] A.C. 614

Commentary

Lord Scarman stated that the basis of economic duress is that it must always amount to a coercion of will, which vitiates consent.

Key Principle: **The right to set the contract aside for economic duress can be lost by affirmation.**

North Ocean Shipping v. Hyundai Construction Co. Ltd, The Atlantic Baron, 1979

D agreed to build a ship for P. The price was to be paid in U.S. dollars over five instalments. After P paid the first instalment, there was a steep decline in the value of the dollar. D demanded a 10 per cent increase in price and threatened not to complete the ship if they were not paid. P agreed. Eight months after completing the payments P claimed repayment of the excess.

Held: (QBD) In principle this was a case of economic duress, since the threat not to build the ship was wrongful and highly coercive of P's will. However, P had lost the right to set the contract aside by not bringing the claim more promptly. [1979] 3 W.L.R. 419

Key Principle: **Economic duress vitiates one party' s consent and renders the contract voidable.**

Universe Tankships of Monrovia v. ITWF, The Universe Sentinel, 1982
Trade union officials threatened to induce the crew of a ship to break their contract of employment so as to prevent the ship leaving port unless P made payments to D's welfare fund. If implemented the threats would have catastrophic financial consequences for shipowners. Therefore it was conceded that the threats amounted to economic duress.

Held: (HL) P's consent to make payments was vitiated by D's economic duress. P could recover the money paid. [1982] 2 W.L.R. 803

Commentary
Thus HL assumed the existence of a doctrine of economic duress based on illegitimate economic pressure.

Key Principle: **Illegitimate pressure will amount to economic duress.**

Dimskal Shipping Co. S.A. v. ITWF 1990
P, shipowners, were coerced into contracting with, and making payments to D, an international trade union, by D's threatened and actual "blacking" of their ship while berthed in a Swedish port.

Held: (CA) P were entitled to avoid the contracts (which were governed by English law) and recover the payments, notwith-standing that the industrial action was permitted under Swedish law. [1990] 1 Lloyd's Rep. 319

Commentary
(1) The court preferred to talk of legitimate or illegitimate pressure not just coercion of will, *i.e.* look at the pressure as well as the effect on the individual.
(2) The case went to the House of Lords in 1991 ([1991] 3 W.L.R. 875) where the main discussion was whether the legality of the industrial action should be determined by English or Swedish law. It was accepted that there was illegitimate pressure.

Key Principle: **The illegitimate pressure vitiates the consent to be bound.**

Atlas v. Kafco 1989
D were under contract to supply baskets to branches of Wool-worths. D entered into a contract with P whereby P would deliver the baskets at an agreed price. However, P over-estimated the number of cartons which could be loaded onto one trailer and had set the price per carton too low. P then tried to vary the price agreed and ultimately stated that unless D agreed to pay a new increased price per load P would not deliver the baskets. D considered that they would be unable to find an alternative carrier. D felt compelled to sign the new agreement, but soon after the deliveries were completed they refused to pay the additional sums on grounds of economic duress.

Held: (QBD) D were not liable to pay the increased price. P put illegitimate pressure amounting to economic duress on D. [1989] 3 W.L.R. 389

Key Principle: **Economic duress would not be proved in the context of arm's length commercial dealing between two companies.**

CTN Cash and Carry v. Gallaher 1994
P bought cigarettes from D who delivered them by mistake to the wrong address, from where they were stolen. D invoiced P

for the cigarettes and threatened to cut off P's credit facilities if
they did not pay. P paid the invoice and then brought an action
to recover the money on the grounds that it had been paid
under economic duress.

Held: (CA) P could not recover the money. Commercial parties are free to withdraw credit facilities without that amounting
to economic duress. [1994] 4 All E.R. 714

Key Principle: **To exert ordinary commercial pressure to
obtain payment is not a breach of Article 82 (formerly 86) of
the E.C. Treaty.**

Leyland Daf Ltd v. Automotive Products Plc 1993
P manufactured motor vehicles but became insolvent, and
receivers were appointed. D supplied parts. P owed D substantial sums of money. D threatened to stop supplying brakes and
clutches if the receiver did not pay P's pre-receivership debts
(which they were not legally obliged to do). In practice there
was no alternative source of supply. If the receivers did not pay
then production would be brought to a halt. The receivers
sought an injunction to compel D to continue to supply parts.

Held: (CA) Under common law principles a court would not
order D to trade with P. Under Article 82 (formerly 86) of the
E.C. Treaty abuse of a dominant position meant using methods
different from normal commercial operations. This was not the
case here. [1993] B.C.C. 389

Unconscionability

Key Principle: **The elements of unconscionability exist in
English law.**

Lloyds Bank v. Bundy 1974
(For facts see p. 110).

Held: (CA) Two of the judges set aside the guarantee on the grounds of undue influence, but Lord Denning suggested that a single thread runs through various categories in English law, including undue influence and undue pressure; that thread is inequality of bargaining power.

Key Principle: **There is no need for a general principle of unconscionability in English law.**

National Westminster Bank v. Morgan 1985

D's family home was owned jointly by H and W(D). It was mortgaged to a building society. H was unable to meet the mortgage repayments and the building society started repossession proceedings. H wanted to remortgage the house to P. A bank manager visited W at home to obtain her signature. W stated that she had no confidence in H's business schemes. The bank manager incorrectly told her that the new mortgage was in effect for the same amount as the old one. In fact the mortgage was to be unlimited so that all of H's liabilities could be charged against the house. W signed the documents. W received no independent legal advice. P claimed possession of the house. W claimed that the mortgage was obtained as a result of P's undue influence.

Held: (HL) A special relationship did not exist between a banker and customer. The mortgage was not obtained as a result of P's undue influence. [1985] 2 W.L.R. 588

Commentary

(1) In Lord Scarman's opinion there is no general principle of inequality of bargaining power in English law. It is relevant in some cases of undue influence. There is no need for a general principle. Where necessary legislation has been enacted to protect the weaker party, *e.g.* U.C.T.A. 1977.

(2) The idea of a general principle has received a more enthusiastic reception in the USA, Australia, and Canada. English courts tend to accept hard but fair bargaining as legitimate.

12. VOID AND ILLEGAL CONTRACTS

Introduction

Key Principle: **A contract which appears legal may be illegal if one party has an illegal purpose in mind.**

Pearce v. Brooks 1866
D hired a new carriage, which was unusually designed, from P. D was a prostitute and she intended to use the carriage to attract customers. P were aware that this was her intention. After paying one instalment D returned the carriage. P sued D for damages under the agreement.

Held: P could not recover the money because P knew that D had hired the carriage to attract customers. [1861–1873] All E.R. Rep. 102

Commentary
(1) If P had not been aware of D's activities they would not have been implicated in the illegality and would have been able to recover damages.
(2) In *Armhouse Lee v. Chappell, The Times,* August 7, 1996 the CA held that the defendants were contractually bound to pay for the placing of telephone sex line advertisements in magazines. The contracts were not immoral or illegal on grounds of public policy.
(3) The law may refuse to give full effect to a contract because the contract involves the commission of a legal wrong or is in some other way contrary to public policy.
(4) There is no agreed classification of such contracts. Generally the important question is what effect does the illegality have on the parties rights. See Law Commission Consultation Paper No. 154, *Illegal Transactions: The Effect of Illegality on Contracts and Trusts* (1999).
(5) This chapter concentrates on one particular type of illegal contract: contracts in restraint of trade. These occur frequently in practice. They are an example of contracts which are void on grounds of public policy.

Key Principle: **Although an illegal contract cannot be enforced by a guilty party, a claim which arises out of the contract, under for example the law of trusts, may be upheld.**

Tinsley v. Milligan 1993
P and D, who were lovers, ran a lodging house as a business. They purchased a new house using money from a previous house. Although the house was in P's sole name, they regarded the house as belonging to both of them. P and D agreed that the house was to be in P's name alone so that D could fraudulently claim money from the Department of Social Security by stating that she did not own a house and that P was her landlady. P and D quarrelled. P moved out of the house and claimed possession. D claimed that the property was held by P on trust for them both in equal shares.

Held: (HL) D had established that a resulting trust existed. She was entitled to recover under the resulting trust. She did not have to rely on the illegal contract, even though the rights she acquired under the trust arose from the performance of the illegal contract. [1993] 3 W.L.R. 126

Commentary
Similarly, if a breach of contract also amounts to a tort a guilty party may be able to recover money by suing in tort.

Key Principle: **A contract in restraint of trade is prima facie void, unless the restriction is reasonable from the point of view of the parties themselves and the public at large.**

Nordenfelt v. Maxim Nordenfelt Guns and Ammunition Co. 1894
D, a manufacturer of guns and other weapons, sold his business to P. The contract provided that D would not for 25 years engage in:

"any business involving the gun trade, or *in any business competing or liable to compete in any way with that for the time being carried on by the company.*"

Held: (HL) The clause was valid except for the part italicised. It was valid because D had sold his gun business, so he should not be able to set up in competition. The clause kept the business in England, which was in the public interest. Nevertheless, the latter part of the clause was too wide and was not necessary to protect P's proprietary interests. That part of the clause was declared void and severed from the contract. [1891–1894] All E.R. Rep. 1

Commentary
(1) The burden of proving that the clause is reasonable rests on the party seeking to uphold the clause.
(2) Note the clause was worldwide in effect.

Key Principle: **A restraint of trade clause is more likely to be upheld in a contract for the sale of a business, than in a contract of employment.**

Mason v. Provident Clothing and Supply Co. Ltd 1913
D, an agent, was employed to canvass for orders and collect debts in Islington. D was not permitted by a clause in his contract with P to trade within 25 miles of London for three years after ceasing employment with P.

Held: (HL) The clause was void. In a contract of employment the employer is normally in a stronger bargaining position than the employee. [1911–1913] All E.R. Rep. 400

Commentary
In a contract for the sale of a business the parties are more likely to be of equal bargaining power. Purchasers need to be able to protect their investment. They buy goodwill, and obtain a proprietary interest.

Key Principle: **A clause which restrains an employee from competition is always void as being unreasonable unless there is some exceptional proprietary interest owned by the employer which needs protection.**

Morris (Herbert) Ltd v. Saxelby 1916
D, an employee, had spent all his working life in the employment of P, which manufactured hoisting machinery in the

United Kingdom. A clause in his contract of employment forbade him from working in a similar business in the United Kingdom and Ireland for seven years after leaving P's employment.

Held: (HL) The clause was void. If upheld it would mean that an employer could force an employee to use a skill developed in his employment exclusively for the benefit of the employer. [1916–1917] All E.R. Rep. 305

Key Principle: **The doctrine of restraint of trade is not limited to contracts for the sale of a business and contracts of employment.**

Esso Petroleum Co Ltd v. Harpers Garage (Stourport) Ltd 1967
D owned two garages. They entered into two solus agreements with P; an agreement for each garage. Both agreements contained the following clauses:

1. a "tying covenant" by which D agreed in return for a discount to sell only P's brand of petrol;

2. a "compulsory trading covenant" which obliged D to keep the garage open at reasonable hours and to provide the public with an efficient service;

3. a "continuity covenant" which required D, if they sold the business, to procure the acceptance of the agreement by the purchaser.

The first agreement was to operate for four years five months and the second for 21 years. In addition under the second agreement the garage was mortgaged to P for £7,000. The mortgage was to be repaid over 21 years and could not be redeemed earlier. D was in breach of the first clause and P sought an injunction to prevent further breaches.

Held: (HL) Both agreements fell within the category of contracts in restraint of trade. D's freedom to trade was limited. The restrictions (1.)—(3.) were reasonable because both parties benefited. However, although the 4½-year period was reasonable the 21–year period was unreasonable because it was excessive and not in the public interest. Therefore, the first agreement was valid, but the second was void. [1967] 1 All E.R. 699

Commentary
(1) The House of Lords considered that the following approach should be used: is the contract/clause so restrictive of the promisor's liberty to trade that it must be treated as prima facie void? If yes, can the clause be justified as reasonable? If yes, then valid.
(2) The court should look at current commercial practice. Solus agreements for garages were not established practice in the trade at this time.
(3) Public interest appears to be the court's notion of what is appropriate, *e.g.* free competition should be encouraged.
(4) Tying agreements are also common in the brewery trade where pubs are "tied houses". These agreements may also be invalid under Article 81 (formerly 85) of the E.C. Treaty. See, for example, *Courage Ltd v. Crehan, The Times,* October 4, 2001 (ECJ).

Contracts for the Sale of a Business

Key Principle: **Some proprietary interest of the purchaser must be protected by the clause.**

British Reinforced Concrete Engineering Co. Ltd v. Schelff 1921
D sold his business making "loop" road reinforcements to P who made BRC road reinforcements. There was a clause to restrain D from making road reinforcements.

Held: (Ch D) The clause was void. P could only stop D making "loop" road reinforcements. Only the actual business sold by D to P was entitled to protection. [1921] 2 Ch. 563

Commentary
(1) When considering the reasonableness of the covenant, the court will also consider the area and duration of the restraint as well as the public interest (*e.g. Nordenfelt v. Maxim Nordenfelt* (1894) see p. 124). See also the cases under contracts of employment below.
(2) It is not uncommon for manufacturers or traders to form an association with the object of restricting the output or maintaining the selling price of certain commodities. At common law such

restrictive trading agreements are subject to the restraint of trade doctrine, but for the most part such agreements are now covered by the Competition Act 1998 (which replaces the Restrictive Trade Practices Act 1976 and the Resale Prices Act 1976) and Article 81 (formerly 85) of the E.C. Treaty.

Key Principle: **In principle covenants in restraint of trade contained in a contract for the sale of a business are subject to Article 81 (formerly 85) of the E.C. Treaty.**

Remia B.V. Verenigde Bedrijven Nutricia NV v. E.C. Commission 1987

Nutricia, a Dutch company sold its sauce business to another Dutch business. It was a term of the agreement that neither N nor another subsidiary would engage directly or indirectly in the production or sale of sauces on the Dutch market for 10 years. N notified the E.C. Commission of this and various other related agreements. N's request for exemption from Article 85 was refused. N appealed against this finding.

Held: (ECJ) The agreement affected inter-state trade although it related to a purely Dutch activity. The 10–year non-competition clause was too long, four years was sufficient. [1987] 1 C.M.L.R. 1

Commentary

Article 81 (formerly 85) treats as invalid all agreements between undertakings which may affect trade between Member States and which have as their object or effect the restriction or distortion of competition within the common market.

Contracts of Employment

Key Principle: **The clause in restraint of trade must protect a legitimate interest of the employer.**

Fitch v. Dewes 1921

D was a solicitor's managing clerk. In his contract of employment there was a lifelong restraint not to practise within seven miles of P's office in Tamworth Town Hall.

Held: The clause was valid because of the contact D had with P's clients. [1921] 2 A.C. 158

Commentary
Where there is an express term in the contract of employment it is more likely to be enforced where it relates to trade secrets and customer information.

Key Principle: **The clause will not be valid if it merely protects an employer against competition from an ex-employee.**

Marshall v. NM Financial Management Ltd 1997
P was a sales agent for D, selling mainly life assurance and pensions. It was a term of P's contract with D that if on termination of the contract P did not become a representative or employee of "any company or organisation which may directly or indirectly be in competition with the company", then D would pay P renewal commission due from business he obtained before the termination.

Held: (CA) The clause was void because it was in restraint of trade. No legitimate interest of the defendant was protected by it. P's business as an agent arose from his reputation and connections and was his property. The anti-competition part of the clause could be severed so that the right to commission remained enforceable. [1997] 1 W.L.R. 1527

Key Principle: **The court will uphold freedom of contract against third parties as well as the parties to the contract.**

Eastham v. Newcastle United Football Club Ltd 1964
P, a football player, entered into a contract with D which provided for the "retain and transfer" system. This meant that D had the right to keep P as a player and that P could not transfer to another club without D's consent.

Held: The clause was void. It neither protected D's trade secrets, nor had P obtained influence over D's customers, the fans. The court issued a declaration not only against D but also against the F.A. [1964] Ch. 413

Commentary
In the *Bosman* case ([1996] All E.R. [E.C.] 97) the European Court of Justice held that National Football Association rules, which prevented a footballer transferring to a football club in another Member State unless the club paid a transfer fee, were in breach of Article 48 (now 39) of the E.C. Treaty on the freedom of movement of workers.

Key Principle: **The clause must be reasonable as to its geographical area.**

Mason v. Provident Clothing and Supply Co. Ltd 1913
See facts at p. 125.

Held: (HL) The clause restricting D's freedom to trade was void. The area covered by the clause was 10,000 times larger than where D was employed. [1911–1913] All E.R. Rep. 400

Key Principle: **The clause must be reasonable as to its duration.**

Fellowes & Son v. Fisher 1976
D, a solicitor's clerk, entered into a contract of employment with P, a firm of solicitors in Walthamstow in east London. A clause of the contract provided that if D left the firm he would not for five years be directly or indirectly employed in the legal profession within the postal districts of Walthamstow and Chingford, an area of 12 square miles with a population of about 150,000. He left his employment and after working in the City of London for six months he obtained a post in Chingford. P applied for an interlocutory injunction to restrain D from breaking the clause.

Held: (CA) The application for an injunction was refused. D was more likely to succeed than P at any full trial. [1976] Q.B. 122

Commentary
It is unlikely that a lifelong restraint in a prescribed area would now be upheld (compare *Fitch v. Dewes*, see p. 128).

Key Principle: **The clause must be reasonable and fair as between the parties.**

Office Angels Ltd v. Rainer-Thomas 1991
D were two employees of P, an employment agency with 34 branches. It was a term of their contracts of employment that:

(a) D would not for six months after the termination of their employment, solicit custom from any person who had been a company client during their employment; and

(b) D would not within six months of their employment engage in or undertake the trade or business of an employment agency in Greater London within a 1km radius of the branch at which they had been employed. D were employed at a branch in the City of London, before leaving to set up their own employment agency within the 1km radius and in the City of London.

Held: (CA) Clause (a) was void. It was too wide because it applied to clients at any of the 34 branches not just the branch where D were employed. Clause (b) was also void. It merely protected P's trade connections with its clients by preventing D from operating an office within the 1km radius. It did not specifically protect P's trade secrets or confidential information. It went further than was reasonable. [1991] I.R.L.R. 214

Commentary
Generally, the court will take into account the adequacy of the consideration in relation to the extent of the restraint, and the relative bargaining strength of the two parties.

Key Principle: **The covenant should not prejudice the public interest.**

Wyatt v. Kreglinger and Fernau 1933
P was a wool broker. When he retired D, his employers, offered him a pension which was conditional upon him not unfairly competing with his former employers. Subsequently he sued to recover arrears of pension.

Held: (CA) The agreement to pay P a pension was in restraint of trade. The clause was unreasonable because it deprived the community of P's services, which might be of benefit to the community. [1933] 1 K.B. 793

Key Principle: **A clause which forfeits pension rights can be void.**

Bull v. Pitney-Bowes Ltd 1966
P, an ex-employee of D, was liable to forfeit pension rights if he engaged in any activity or occupation which was in competition with or detrimental to the interests of D.

Held: (Ch D) The clause was void on grounds of public policy It is contrary to public policy to deprive the community of a person's skills. [1967] 1 W.L.R. 273

Commentary
See also *Marshall v. NM Financial Management Ltd* (see p. 129).

Key Principle: **If an employer, in breach of contract, dismisses an employee then a covenant in restraint of trade cannot be enforced by the employer.**

Briggs v. Oates 1991
D, a solicitor, was employed by P and his partner in a firm of solicitors. It was a clause of D's contract of employment that D would not for five years after its termination practise as a solicitor within five miles of the firm's offices or solicit any persons who were clients of the firm while he was employed

there. The partnership was dissolved and D obtained alternative employment which was in breach of the clause.

Held: (QBD) P's application for an injunction was refused. The dissolution of the partnership was a breach of D's contract of employment and brought it to an end, so the clause was no longer binding on D. [1991] 1 All E.R. 407

Key Principle: **There is an implied duty of fidelity in every contract of employment.**

Faccenda Chicken v. Fowler 1986

P, a company, marketed fresh chickens. P employed D as a sales manager. D devised a marketing system for P. D left P's company, and set up a similar business in the same area employing a number of P's staff. There was no express clause in D's contract of employment which restricted the activities of P's former employees. P applied for injunction to restrain D from using confidential sales information.

Held: (CA) P's application was not successful. Sales information was not a trade secret, and therefore was not protected. [1986] 3 W.L.R. 288

Commentary
(1) The court considered that:

  (a) Ex-employees do not owe the same duty of fidelity as a current employee in relation to information short of trade secrets (unless that information could be memorised or recorded). Such information could not be protected in any event.

  (b) In deciding whether information amounts to a trade secret, the court should take into account:

     (i) the nature of the employment and the status of the employee;

     (ii) the nature of the information;

     (iii) whether the employer had stressed the confidentiality of the information to the employee; and

(iv) whether the information could be collated from other non-confidential information.

(2) An express clause will more readily be applied to ex-employees.

Partnership Agreements

Key Principle: **The restraint of trade doctrine applies to partnership agreements.**

Bridge v. Deacons 1984
A solicitors' partnership agreement contained a clause whereby a party who ceased to be a partner was restricted for five years thereafter from acting as a solicitor in Hong Kong for any client of the firm either at the time he ceased to be a partner or during the preceding three years.

Held: (JCPC) P, the firm of solicitors, could enforce the clause against D. It was not in restraint of trade. The clause applied to all of the partners. A five-year period was not unreasonable. The consideration paid for D's share of the partnership was adequate. The system for acquiring and relinquishing a share of the partnership was reasonable and in the public interest. [1984] 2 W.L.R. 837

Key Principle: **An injunction may be obtained to prevent a former member of a partnership practising in breach of the partnership agreement.**

Clarke v. Newland 1991
P was a medical practitioner in general practice in central London. In 1982 D joined P as an assistant GP. D became a partner in October 1985. It was a term of the partnership agreement that D undertook not to practise in the practice area within a period of three years in the event of the agreement being terminated. Subsequently the partnership was terminated and D set up in general practice 100 yards from P's surgery.

Held: (CA) P was granted an injunction against D. The clause was not too wide. To "practise" meant practise as a GP. [1991] 1 All E.R. 397

Exclusive Service Agreements

Key Principle: **An exclusive service agreement is subject to the doctrine of restraint of trade.**

A. Schroeder Music Publishing Co. Ltd v. Macaulay 1974

P, a young and unknown song-writer, entered into a contract with D, a music publishing company, on D's standard terms. Under the contract, P assigned the world copyright in his musical compositions to D who did not undertake to exploit all or indeed any of them. D would pay P royalties if D did exploit them. The five-year agreement could be automatically extended by D for a further five years if P's royalties reached £5,000. D could terminate the agreement at any time on giving one month's notice. P had no such right.

Held: (HL) Such an agreement fell within the doctrine of restraint of trade. The contract was unreasonable because it was very one-sided. [1974] 1 W.L.R. 1308

Commentary
(See also p. 56).

Key Principle: **Where the terms of an agreement are prescribed by an outside body then such a contract is subject to the restraint of trade doctrine.**

Watson v. Prager 1991

P was a professional boxer. He entered into a British Boxing Board of Control boxer-manager agreement with D for three years. D had the right to P's exclusive services. D was also a boxing promoter. The agreement provided that:

(a) D had a right to extend the contract for a further three years if P won a championship fight;

(b) D could stipulate the terms on which P would fight matches.

Held: (Ch D) The clauses were unreasonable because D could impose on P the terms on which he had to fight, and the option to renew was for too long a period. [1991] 1 W.L.R. 726

Key Principle: **An exclusive services agreement will not be in restraint of trade where the parties are of equal bargaining power.**

Panayiotou v. Sony Music Entertainment (U.K.) 1994
In 1988 P, George Michael (Panayiotou), entered into an agreement with CBS Records whereby he agreed to: deliver eight albums of music in 15 years; only record for CBS; and receive around 20 per cent of the sale price in royalties. CBS obtained copyright to the work, but were under no obligation to promote it. CBS's recording business was then taken over by D. P claimed that the contract he entered into was void because it was an unreasonable restraint of trade, and it was void under Article 85(2) of the E.C. Treaty.

Held: (Ch D) It was not in restraint of trade because:

(a) P had received expert legal advice from his solicitors at all times.

(b) there was a public interest in upholding a compromise such as the 1988 agreement.

(c) P had affirmed the agreement in 1990 when he obtained an advance payment.

(d) there was no breach of Article 85 because there was no Community-wide market for the services of U.K. recording artists in the field of popular music and so the agreement did not affect trade between Member States. The relevant market for P's services was the U.K. market not a Community-wide market. *The Times*, June 30, 1994

Franchise Agreements

Key Principle: **A franchisor is entitled to protect the goodwill of the business by preventing a franchisee setting up in competition with the franchised business.**

Kall-Kwik Printing (U.K.) Limited v. Rush 1996
In 1983 P entered into a twenty-year franchise agreement with D. It was a term of the agreement that for two years after the

expiry of the agreement D would not engage in any business, within a ten mile radius of the franchised business, which competed with it. In 1995 D set up a similar business less than a mile from the original premises, and subsequently terminated the franchise agreement.

Held: The restriction upon competition by D was reasonable. [1996] F.S.R. 114.

Severance

Key Principle: **Where the contract is partly void and partly valid then the court may sever the void part of the contract provided that it does not contain the whole or substantially the whole consideration for the contract.**

Marshall v. NM Financial Management Ltd 1995
(For facts see p. 129).

Held: (CA) The question as to consideration was one of substance not form. The two clauses in restraint of trade could be struck out (although only the first was of relevance to P). The remainder of the contract was valid, and so P could recover the post termination commission to which he was entitled under the contract.

Commentary
(1) This is known as the "Blue pencil" test.
(2) The courts also severed the void clause in, *e.g. Nordenfelt v. Maxim Nordenfelt Guns and Amunition Co., British Reinforced Concrete Engineering Co. Ltd v. Schelff* (see pp. 124 and 127).

13. DISCHARGE BY AGREEMENT AND BY FRUSTRATION

By Agreement

Key Principle: **Unless there is fresh consideration for a promise to release one party from their obligations, the promise to release will not be enforceable.**

Foakes v. Beer 1884
P had obtained judgment against D for £2,090. However, she
agreed to allow D to pay her by instalments and not to take any
proceedings to enforce the judgment. A judgment debt attracts
interest from the date of the judgment. D paid the debt, but P
then claimed the interest.

Held: (HL) P was entitled to recover the interest (see p. 30).
[1881–1885] All E.R. Rep. 106

Commentary
(1) If P had agreed to forgo the interest and D had provided
consideration for her promise this would be an example of
unilateral discharge.
(2) A contract can be terminated in the same way as it is created.
When a contract is entered into there has to be "agreement" and
"consideration", and similarly when a contract is ended by agreement there has to be "accord" and "satisfaction".

Key Principle: **A promise not to insist on exact performance
may be effective as a waiver, even without consideration.**

Hughes v. Metropolitan Railway 1877
In October 1874 a landlord gave his tenant six months' notice to
repair the property. In November the landlord started negotiations to buy the remainder of the lease from the tenant. The
negotiations broke down in December. The tenant did not carry
out any repairs. At the end of the six-month period the landlord
claimed that the lease was forfeited.

Held: The landlord was not entitled to forfeit the lease. The
tenant had failed to carry out the repairs because the landlord
had started negotiations to buy the remainder of the lease.
(1877) 2 App. Cas. 439

Commentary
(1) The tenant had not provided any consideration for the landlord's promise. The landlord's right to forfeit was suspended not
lost.
(2) The equitable principle of waiver was used to support the
creation of the doctrine of promissory estoppel (see *High Trees*
case, p. 32, above.).

Key Principle: **A promise not to insist on exact performance can be revoked by giving reasonable notice.**

Charles Rickards v. Oppenheim 1950

In July 1947 D agreed to take delivery of a new Rolls Royce car from P within "six months or, at the most, seven months". The car was not ready in time and D agreed to wait another three months. When it was still not ready then D gave notice that if the car was not ready within four weeks he would cancel the order, which he did.

Held: (CA) D was entitled to refuse to take delivery of the car. Although he had waived his right to take delivery of the car by a particular date, he had reasserted this right when requiring the car to be ready within four weeks. [1950] 1 All E.R. 420

Commentary
(1) P were in breach of contract by failing to deliver the car on time. The court considered that "time was of the essence", which meant that D was entitled to treat the contract as discharged or terminated by P's failure to deliver on time.
(2) Denning L.J. considered that D's waiver was a type of estoppel similar to that in the *High Trees* case (see p. 32). D was entitled by the giving of reasonable notice to make time of the essence once again.

Key Principle: **Discharge by agreement may be inferred from prolonged inactivity in certain circumstances.**

The Hannah Blumenthal 1983

In 1972 the buyers of a ship referred a dispute with the sellers to arbitration in accordance with the contract of sale. Letters were occasionally exchanged between the parties until 1980 when the buyers proposed fixing a date for the arbitration hearing. The sellers claimed that the arbitration agreement had been discharged by a mutual agreement to abandon the arbitration.

Held: (HL) Whether or not a contract is abandoned is a question of fact, and in this case there was no mutual agreement to abandon the arbitration agreement. [1983] 1 All E.R. 34

Commentary
(1) Where two parties agree to release each other from their respective obligations under a contract this is a bilateral discharge.
(2) In this case their Lordships agreed that there could be "tacit abandonment by both parties". However, three different views were expressed as to what would amount to "tacit abandonment". Lord Brightman's view reflects the traditional objective approach to contract formation. He considered that the sellers must show that the buyers so conducted themselves as to entitle the sellers to assume, and that the sellers did assume, that the contract was to be abandoned without any further communication.

By Frustration

Key Principle: **Frustration occurs where a contractual obligation has become incapable of being performed because external circumstances have caused the performance to be radically different from that agreed.**

Davis Contractors Ltd v. Fareham Urban District Council 1956
P contractors agreed to build 78 houses for D for £92,425 within eight months. Due to a shortage of skilled labour and building materials the work took 22 months and cost £111,076. P claimed that the contract was frustrated by the long delay and claimed the additional costs on a *quantum meruit* basis.

Held: (HL) The contract was not frustrated because the cause of the delay was not unforeseeable, and delay did not have the same significance for both parties. [1956] 3 W.L.R. 37

Commentary
(1) The change in circumstances should not be the fault of either party.
(2) "Frustration is not to be lightly invoked as the dissolvent of a contract", *per* Lord Radcliffe.

Key Principle: **The doctrine of frustration will apply to leases, but only in exceptional circumstances.**

National Carriers v. Panalpina 1981
In January 1974 P leased a warehouse to D for 10 years. In May 1979 the local authority closed the only access road to the

warehouse because of the dangerous condition of a listed building. The closure was likely to last 18 months. P claimed rent due. D claimed the lease was frustrated by the closure.

Held: (HL) The denial of access to the warehouse was not sufficiently serious to frustrate the contract. [1981] 2 W.L.R. 45

Commentary
(1) Lord Hailsham considered that the shorter the lease the more likely it would be that the doctrine would be applicable.
(2) If a hotel was built on a cliff which slipped into the North Sea and the property was leased then the lease would be frustrated.

Key Principle: **Where performance of the contract becomes impossible because of the destruction of the subject-matter of the contract then the contract is frustrated.**

Taylor v. Caldwell 1863
D hired out the Surrey Gardens and Music Hall to P for a series of concerts. Six days before the first concert the Hall was destroyed by an accidental fire.

Held: D was not liable to P for wasted advertising and other expenses. (1863) 122 E.R. 309

Commentary
(1) The court's view was that there was an implied term in the contract that excused the parties.
(2) The destruction of something other than the subject-matter of the contract will still cause the contract to be discharged by frustration if the result is that the main purpose of the contract is defeated.

Key Principle: **Where performance of the contract becomes impossible because a person or object which is essential for performance is unavailable then the contract may be frustrated.**

The Evia (No. 2) 1982
In November 1979 P, the owners of the ship, chartered their vessel to D for 18 months. In September 1980 the ship unloaded

its cargo in Basrah but was detained in the Shatt-Al-Arab
waterway because of the outbreak of the Iran/Iraq war. The
ship was still trapped in July 1982 when HL heard the case. D
claimed that the charterparty had been frustrated when it
became clear that the hostilities would not be shortlived. P
claimed that D were in breach of the charterparty by sending
the ship to Basrah when it was not "a safe port".

Held: (HL) D were not in breach of the charterparty. The
decision of the lower courts, that the performance of the
charterparty became impossible and the contract was frustrated
on October 4, 1980, was accepted. [1982] 3 All E.R. 350

Commentary
See also *Jackson v. Union Marine Insurance Co. Ltd* (1874) which
involved a voyage charter rather than a time charter. A ship was
chartered by D for a voyage from Liverpool to San Francisco via
Newport where a cargo was to be loaded. The ship ran aground
before arriving at Newport. It took more than eight months for
the ship to be refloated and repaired. The court held that the
voyage the parties contemplated had become impossible. There
was an implied condition that the ship should arrive in time to
load the cargo. (1874) L.R. 10 C.P. 125

Key Principle: **Where the method of performance of the
contract becomes impossible then the contract is frustrated.**

Nickoll & Knight v. Ashton Edridge & Co. 1901
In a contract for the sale of cottonseed, it was provided that the
cottonseed would be shipped on a named ship from a specified
port during a particular month. Before the loading date the ship
went aground.

Held: (CA) Since the contract did not provide for any alternative method of performance, *e.g.* a different ship, the contract
was frustrated. [1901] 2 K.B. 126

Key Principle: **Where substituted performance is possible under the contract, then the contract is not frustrated.**

Tsakiroglou & Co. Ltd v. Noblee Thorl 1961
P agreed to buy groundnuts from D, who was to ship them to Hamburg from Port Sudan. It was contemplated by both parties that the ship would use the Suez canal. The canal was then closed to shipping, and the sellers did not deliver the goods claiming that the contract was frustrated.

Held: (HL) The contract was not frustrated. The goods could have been shipped via the Cape of Good Hope, which would not have been commercially or fundamentally different from what was agreed. [1961] 2 W.L.R. 633

Key Principle: **Where a change in circumstances radically affects the purpose of the contract then the contract will be frustrated.**

Krell v. Henry 1903
D hired rooms in Pall Mall for two days in order to see Edward VII's coronation procession as it passed along Pall Mall. No reference to the procession was made in the written agreement. The coronation was postponed because of the king's illness.

Held: (CA) The contract was frustrated. The taking place of the processions was regarded by both parties as being the foundation or basis of the contract, and their postponement prevented performance of the contract. [1903] 2 K.B. 740

Commentary
See also Chandler v. Webster (1904) (see p. 147).

Key Principle: **A change in circumstances which only incidentally affects the purpose of the contract will not frustrate the contract.**

Herne Bay Steamboat Co. v. Hutton 1903
D chartered a steamboat from P in order to take paying passengers to see the royal naval review at Spithead and for a

day's cruise round the fleet. The naval review was cancelled because of the king's illness.

Held: (CA) The naval review was not the foundation of the contract so the contract was not frustrated when it was cancelled. [1900–1903] All E.R. Rep. 627

Commentary
See also *WJ Tatem Ltd v. Gamboa* (1938) (see p. 145)

Key Principle: **A change in circumstances which makes the contract impracticable for one party will not frustrate the contract.**

British Movietonews Ltd v. London & District Cinemas Ltd 1952
During the Second World War P and D entered into an agreement for the supply of newsreels. D argued that the contract was frustrated because the war was over and there was no longer any need to show these particular newsreels.

Held: (HL) The contract was not frustrated just because it was no longer commercially viable for one party. [1952] A.C. 166

Key Principle: **If a valid contract becomes illegal because of a change in the law then the contract is frustrated.**

Fibrosa Spolka Akcyjnia v. Fairbairn Lawson Combe Barbour Ltd 1944
In July 1939 D sold machinery to P, a Polish company in Gdynia. An advance payment of £1,000 was paid. In September 1939, before the machinery was due to be delivered, Great Britain declared war on Germany and Germany occupied Gdynia. P requested the return of the £1,000, but D refused because they had carried out a considerable amount of work on the machinery.

Held: (HL) The contract was frustrated because when war is declared it becomes illegal to trade with the enemy. P was entitled to recover the £1,000 because there had been total failure of consideration. [1942] 2 All E.R. 122

Limitations

Key Principle: **Foreseen or foreseeable circumstances which interfere with the performance of the contract will not amount to frustration.**

Davis Contractors Ltd v. Fareham Urban District Council 1956
P claimed that the contract was frustrated because of the long delay in building the houses. (See p. 140 for fuller facts).

Held: (HL) The contract was not frustrated. The shortage of skilled labour and building materials was not unforeseeable. [1956] 3 W.L.R. 37

Commentary
(1) P should have included in the contract a term which provided for additional costs to be paid in the event of delay.
(2) See also *Amalgamated Investment and Property Co. Ltd v. John Walker & Sons Ltd* (1976) (see p. 97) where the court rejected the claim that the contract was frustrated, on the ground that the parties were aware that there was a risk that the building might be listed.
(3) If the contract makes provision for frustrating events, *e.g.* through a *force majeure* clause, or a hardship clause then the doctrine does not apply.

Key Principle: **Circumstances must be actually foreseen or there must be a high degree of forseeability for the doctrine of frustration not to apply.**

WJ Tatem Ltd v. Gamboa 1938
During the Spanish Civil War D chartered a ship for 30 days for the purpose of evacuating the civilian population from northern Spain. 14 days into the charter the Nationalists seized the ship, which was not returned to P for more than eight weeks.

Held: (KBD) The parties had not provided for this eventuality in the contract, even though they had foreseen the possibility of seizure. The foundation of the contract was destroyed and so the contract was frustrated. [1938] 3 All E.R. 135.

Key Principle: **Self-induced frustration will not discharge the contract.**

J Lauritzen A.S. v. Wijsmuller BV, The "Super Servant Two" 1990
D contracted to transport P's oil rig from Japan to Holland using either the "Super Servant One" or the "Super Servant Two" transportation unit. D intended to use the Super Servant Two but it sank. Meanwhile D had allocated the "Super Servant One" to other contracts.

Held: (CA) Where a contract provides for alternative methods of performance, it will not be frustrated if one of them becomes impossible. The contract was not brought to an end automatically by the sinking of the unit but by the decision of D not to use the Super Servant One. [1990] 1 Lloyd's L.R. 1

Commentary
Self-induced frustration would also occur where the transportation unit had been sunk deliberately by D or as a result of D's negligence.

Key Principle: **The burden of proving that the frustration is self-induced is on the party claiming it.**

Joseph Constantine Steamship Line Ltd v. Imperial Smelting Corporation Ltd 1941
P chartered D's steamship. Before a cargo could be loaded a masssive explosion occurred which, it was accepted, frustrated the charterparty. If the explosion was the fault of D then the frustration would have been self-induced, and P would be able to recover damages for breach of the charterparty.

Held: (JCPC) D, as the party pleading the defence of frustration, did not have to prove that it was not self-induced. The onus of proof was on P. [1941] 2 All E.R. 165.

The Effect of Frustration on the Contract

Key Principle: At common law rights accrued under the contract before the frustrating event were enforceable.

Chandler v. Webster 1904
P hired a room for one day in order to see Edward VII's coronation procession. The hire charge of £141.75 was payable immediately. P paid £100. The coronation was postponed because of the King's illness.

Held: (CA) The contract was frustrated. P was unable to recover the £100 and was liable to pay the remaining £41.75 to D. [1904] 1 K.B. 493

Commentary
(1) Frustration releases the parties from further performance after the frustrating event.
(2) The House of Lords in the Fibrosa case (see p. 144) distinguished this case stating that the principle does not apply where there is total failure of consideration.
(3) The Law Reform (Frustrated Contracts) Act 1943, s.1(2) now provides that all sums paid or payable before the frustrating event cease to be payable. Most contracts fall within the statute, but some, for example charterparties, are still governed by the common law rules: section 2(5).

Key Principle: The court has a broad discretion under the proviso in Law Reform (Frustrated Contracts) Act 1943, s.1(2) in deciding whether to recompense a party who has incurred expenses before the frustrating event.

Gamerco S.A. v. ICM/Fair Warning (Agency) Ltd 1995
P, Spanish pop concert promoters, entered into a contract with D, whereby the group Guns n' Roses would perform at a stadium in Madrid on July 4, 1992. On June 30 engineers found structural defects in the stadium. On July 1 the Spanish authorities banned the use of the stadium and revoked the permit to hold the event. P had paid D $412,500 on account. Both P and D had incurred expenses in preparation for the event. P sued under section 1(2) to recover the advance payment.

Held: (QBD) The contract was frustrated because the stadium was unsafe and its use banned. P was entitled to recover the advance payment. Bearing in mind the extent of P's loss no deduction would be made to cover the expenses incurred by D before the frustrating event. [1995] 1 W.L.R. 1226

Commentary
In exercising the discretion under the proviso the judge rejected total retention of expenses by D or equal division of the expenses between the parties. This was the first case to consider the exercise of the discretion.

Key Principle: **At common law money payable under the contract after the frustrating event need not be paid.**

Appleby v. Myers 1867
P agreed to install machinery on D's premises at a cost of £459. When most of the work had been done, an accidental fire destroyed the premises and the machinery. P sued to recover £419 for the work done and materials provided.

Held: Both parties were excused from further performance, which meant that D were not obliged to pay P anything. (1867) L.R. 2 C.P. 651

Commentary
The Law Reform (Frustrated Contracts) Act 1943, s.1(3) now provides that where one party has received a valuable benefit (other than money) before the frustrating event, the court has a discretion to award a just sum not exceeding the "benefit" received by the other party.

Key Principle: **The "valuable benefit" in Law Reform (Frustrated Contracts) Act 1943, s.1(3) should be valued after the frustrating event.**

B.P. Exploration Co. (Libya) Ltd v. Hunt (No. 2) 1979
D owned an oil concession in Libya, half of which he transferred to B.P. in return for oil, cash and a share of the revenues if oil

was found and exploited. B.P. was to fund all the development costs, but D would reimburse B.P. their costs from his share of any revenues. D found a large oilfield, but five years after it came on stream the Libyan government expropriated B.P.'s interest which frustrated the contract between D and B.P. B.P. claimed a "just sum" under section 1(3).

Held: (QBD) B.P. could recover $35 million as the just sum, being the costs which had not been reimbursed by D at the date of the expropriation. [1979] 1 W.L.R. 783

Commentary
(1) The valuable benefit which D received was about $85 million, being the development of the concession by B.P. together with the oil and cash he received.
(2) This is the only case on section 1(3).

14. DISCHARGE BY PERFORMANCE AND BY BREACH

By Performance

Key Principle: **A contract is only discharged by exact performance.**

Bolton v. Mahadeva 1972
P contracted to install a central heating and hot water system in D's house for £560. He installed the system but it did not heat the house properly and gave out noxious fumes. The cost of remedying the defects was estimated at £174. D refused to pay the agreed price.

Held: (CA) P could recover nothing. The contract was not substantially performed. [1972] 1 W.L.R. 1009

Commentary
(1) The remedy for failure to perform puts the parties to the contract in the position they would have been in if the contract had not been made. (See also *Appleby v. Myers* (1867)) (see p. 148).

(2) P had refused to remedy the defects, if he had then he could have recovered the agreed price.

(3) This was an "entire" contract, that is payment was only made when P completed the work. P should have made it a term of the contract that a deposit and/or stage payments were made by D. If such payments had been made D would not have been able to recover them because there would not have been a total failure of consideration.

Key Principle: **Where there has been substantial but not exact performance the other party must still perform their side of the agreement.**

Hoenig v. Isaacs 1952
P agreed to redecorate and furnish D's flat for £750. D paid P £400 but refused to pay the balance because there were minor defects in the work. These would have cost £55 to remedy.

Held: (CA) There was substantial compliance with the contract. D must pay the contract price subject to a deduction of £55 being made, which was the cost of remedying the defects. [1952] 2 All E.R. 176

Commentary
(1) D considered that P should claim compensation on a *quantum meruit* basis. This would amount to a reasonable price for the work done, and may well have been less than the contract price.
(2) P was in breach of contract, but the breach was not sufficiently serious to discharge the contract (see p. 151). It merely enabled D to claim damages.
(3) In most cases failure to perform and breach are two ways of looking at the same circumstances. It is possible for a failure to perform not to amount to a breach.

Key Principle: **Where the promisee has the option to and does accept partial performance, they are bound to pay a reasonable price for what they received.**

Sumpter v. Hedges 1898
P agreed to build two houses and stables for D. The work was partially completed when P ran out of money. D completed the work at his own expense. P sued for the work done.

Held: (CA) P could not recover anything for the work done. He had abandoned the contract. D had no option but to accept the partial performance. He could not be expected to leave the buildings half-finished. [1898] 1 Q.B. 673

Commentary
(1) If D does have a choice, and does accept partial performance, then a new contract arises with the implication that D will pay for the work which had been done on a *quantum meruit* basis, *i.e.* pay a reasonable price.
(2) Building contracts are often broken down into "divisible covenants". Instead of a single payment being made when the entire contract is completed, stage payments are made, *e.g.* when the foundations are laid, the walls built, etc. The obligation is for substantial performance of each covenant.

By Breach

Key Principle: **Breach of a condition gives the injured party the right to treat the contract as repudiated.**

The Mihalis Angelos 1970
In a charterparty P, the shipowner, stated that the ship would be ready to load on about July 1, 1965. D, the charterer, had the option of cancelling the charter if the ship was not ready to load by July 20. D cancelled the charter on July 17 because they did not have a cargo.

Held: (CA) D were entitled to treat the contract as repudiated in July 17. The "expected ready to load" term was a condition for four reasons: certainty in the law; the shipowner would as a result rarely suffer any injustice from this conclusion; in a contract for the sale of goods to be carried at sea such a term was treated as a condition; and this is the view expressed in Scrutton on Charterparties. [1970] 3 W.L.R. 601

Commentary
(1) A contract can be discharged by breach where the injured party has the right to repudiate or rescind the contract. Rescind in this context is different to the equitable remedy of rescission, *e.g.* for misrepresentation.
(2) The injured party is not obliged to repudiate, and can usually choose to affirm the contract instead (see p. 157).

Key Principle: **Whether a term is a condition or not depends upon the intention of the parties.**

Bunge Corporation v. Tradax Export 1981
A contract for the sale of soya bean flour required the buyers to give the sellers at least 15 consecutive days' notice that a ship was ready to load the flour. The sellers then had to nominate a Gulf port.The buyer gave less than 15 days notice. The seller repudiated the contract and claimed damages because the market value of the flour had dropped.

Held: (HL) The obligation to give 15 days notice was a condition. The intention of the parties is determined by looking at the contract and the surrounding circumstances. [1981] 1 W.L.R. 711

Commentary
(1) In mercantile contracts usually "time is of the essence" which means that a term as to time is treated as a condition. In other contracts time clauses are normally treated as warranties, unless the parties intend otherwise.
(2) Lord Wilberforce stated that the courts should not be too ready to interpret contract terms as conditions. He commended the more flexible approach adopted in *Hong Kong Fir Shipping Co. Ltd v. Kawasaki Kisen Kaisha Ltd* (1962), but considered that the courts should first look at the intention of the parties.

Key Principle: **Using the word "condition" within a particular term of a contract does not automatically make that term a "condition" in the legal sense.**

L. Schuler A.G. v. Wickman Machine Tool Sales Ltd 1974
Schuler (D) granted P sole selling rights for D's machinery. Clause 7(b) of the agreement stated that it was a "condition of this agreement" that P's representatives should visit the six largest U.K. motor manufacturers at least once a week to obtain orders. P were in breach of Clause 7(b) and D repudiated the contract. P claimed damages for wrongful repudiation.

Held: (HL) D were not entitled to treat the contract as repudiated. Looking at the contract as a whole Clause 7(b) was not intended to be a "condition" in the legal sense. [1974] A.C. 235

Commentary
Note that "condition" has various meanings including "condition precedent". See, *e.g. Total Gas Marketing Ltd v. Arco British Ltd, The Times,* June 8, 1998, where the HL held that buyers of North Sea gas were entitled to terminate the contract where the sellers failed to comply with such a condition.

Key Principle: **In a contract for the sale of goods if some of the goods do not correspond with the contract description then the buyer usually has the right to reject all the goods.**

Re Moore & Co. and Landauer & Co. 1921
S agreed to sell tinned fruit to B in cases containing 30 tins. The agreed number of tins was supplied but about half the cases contained 24 rather than 30 tins.

Held: (CA) B could reject the whole consignment. [1921] 2 K.B. 519

Commentary
(1) The court was influenced by the fact that the cases may have been brought for subsequent resale which would have involved repacking to obtain the correct number of tins.
(2) The Sale of Goods Acts 1893 and 1979 provided that terms in contracts for the sale of goods were either conditions or warranties. A breach of warranty does not allow the injured party to terminate the contract, only to claim damages. This dichotomy is used by the courts in many other types of contracts. However, the innominate term approach can also be used in contracts for the sale of goods (*Cehave v. Bremer* (1975) (see p. 145)).
(3) Section 13(1) and section 13 (1A) of the Sale of Goods Act 1979 provide that where there is a contract for the sale of goods there is an implied condition that the goods will correspond with the description. However, section 15A removes the right of a business buyer to reject the goods where the breach is so slight that it would be unreasonable for the buyer to do so. The buyer will only be able to claim damages for breach of warranty.

Key Principle: **If the subject-matter of the contract fails to correspond with its description then the buyer should only have the right to reject if there is also a substantial failure of performance.**

Reardon Smith Line v. Hansen-Tangen 1976

P chartered a tanker to D. The ship was to be built by a Japanese company. In the charterparty the ship was identified as Osaka No. 354, but the company sub-contracted the work to the Oshima yard where it was described as Oshima 004. The tanker market collapsed and D wanted to cancel the contract, so they claimed that the tanker did not comply with its contract description.

Held: (HL) D were not entitled to reject the tanker. The breach was technical, it did not amount to substantial failure of performance. [1976] 1 W.L.R. 989

Commentary

This case reintroduced the need for substantial failure of performance (see p. 155) into the condition/warranty analysis of contract terms, and threw doubt on Re Moore and Landauer & Co. (1921) (see p. 153). Section 15(A) of the Sale of Goods Act 1979 reflects this change of approach.

Key Principle: **Where a breach of a term amounts to a substantial failure of performance, the injured party has the right to treat the contract as repudiated.**

Poussard v. Spiers 1876

P, a singer, agreed with D that she would play the leading role in an opera for a three-month period. P became seriously ill five days before the first performance, and it was uncertain how long her illness would last. D found a replacement and refused to take P back when she was better after 11 days.

Held: D were entitled to treat the contract as discharged by P's breach. (1876) 1 QBD 410

Commentary

(1) The court accepted that it was not possible for D to find a temporary replacement just to cover the period of P's illness.

(2) The court looked at the effect of P's "failure of performance" on D.

(3) The obligation on P to perform has also been categorised as a "condition" (see p. 151).

Key Principle: **Where a breach does not amount to a substantial failure of performance, the injured party does not usually have the right to treat the contract as discharged.**

Bettini v. Gye 1876
P, a singer, agreed with D that he would play tenor roles during the 1875 Covent Garden season, which ran from the end of March to the middle of July. In breach of a contract term that he should be present six days before the first performance for rehearsals, P arrived three days late because of illness. D terminated P's contract.

Held: P could still substantially perform his contract. D was not entitled to treat the contract as discharged by P's late arrival. (1876) 1 QBD 183

Commentary
The obligation on P to be present for the rehearsals has also been categorised as a "warranty".

Key Principle: **Where a breach of an innominate term deprives an injured party of substantially the whole benefit of the contract that party is entitled to treat the contract as repudiated.**

Hong Kong Fir Shipping Co. Ltd v. Kawasaki Kisen Kaisha Ltd 1962
P chartered a ship to D for 24 months. P undertook to supply a seaworthy ship. However, the engine room staff were inefficient and the engines were old. During the first four months the ship was delayed by repairs for five weeks. Further repairs which would take 15 weeks to complete were then found to be necessary. D repudiated the contract, and P sued for wrongful repudiation.

Held: P's undertaking as to seaworthiness was neither a condition or a warranty, but an innominate term. D was not entitled to repudiate the contract because P's breach did not deprive D of substantially the whole benefit of the charterparty. [1962] 2 Q.B. 26

Commentary
(1) Lord Diplock's view was that many terms cannot be categorised as conditions or warranties. Such terms are "innominate". (*Bunge v. Tradax*, (see p. 152)).
(2) This results in "the wait and see" approach, *i.e.* the injured party will only know whether breach of a particular term entitles them to repudiate once the effect of the breach is known. Although this approach avoids the rigidity of the condition/warranty dichotomy it can cause uncertainty.

***

Key Principle: **The innominate term approach can be used where there is a contract for the sale of goods.**

Cehave NV v. Bremer, The Hansa Nord 1975
B purchased from S for £100,000 citrus pulp pellets for making cattle-feed. It was a term of the agreement that the shipment would be made "in good condition". When the pellets were unloaded from the ship it was found that part of the shipment had been damaged by overheating. B rejected the whole shipment. The Rotterdam court ordered the sale of the pellets which B indirectly bought for £30,000 and used as originally planned.

Held: (CA) The obligation to ship "in good condition" was not a condition. Its breach did not substantially deprive B of substantially the whole benefit of the contract. [1975] 3 All E.R. 739

Commentary
The pellets were held to be of merchantable quality as defined by section 14 of the Sale of Goods Act 1893. The Sale of Goods Act 1893 dichotomy did not exclude the innominate term or intermediate stipulation approach.

***

Key principle: **The innominate term approach is applicable to a long-term contract for the provision of services**

Rice (t/a The Garden Guardian) v. Great Yarmouth Borough Council 2000

In February 1996 P entered into a four-year contract to provide leisure management and grounds maintenance services. The contract provided that P should "provide the service in a proper skilful and workmanlike manner to the contract standard and to the entire satisfaction of [D]", and that D could terminate the contract for the breach of any term by P. In August 1996 D terminated the contract because P failed to comply with a number of contractual obligations, for example, complete the summer bedding and renovate certain football pitches by specific dates. P sued D for money due under the contract.

Held: (CA) Where there is a long-running contract to provide public services the question for the court is whether the cumulative effect of the breaches of contract complained of is so serious as to justify the innocent party in bringing the contract to a premature end. On the facts P's claim should succeed because D was not entitled to terminate the contract (unreported).

Commentary
(1) This appears to be the first CA case considering termination of such a contract.
(2) Hale L.J. stated that this is a classic example of an innominate term: one which can be broken in so many different ways and with such varying consequences that the parties cannot be taken to have intended that any breach should entitle the innocent party to terminate the whole contract.

Key Principle: **The right of an injured party to affirm the contract after a repudiatory breach is not absolute.**

White & Carter (Councils) Ltd v. McGregor 1962

P entered into a three-year contract with D to make litter bins advertising D's business, but D cancelled the contract the same day. P refused to accept the wrongful repudiation by D and made the bins as agreed. P sued D for all the money due under the contract. D claimed that P were only entitled to damages for breach of contract.

Held: (HL) P were entitled to affirm the contract even though affirmation did not benefit them particularly, and caused D greater loss than a claim for damages would have done. [1962] 2 W.L.R. 17

Commentary

The decision was a 3:2 majority. Lord Reid who was one of the majority considered that the right to affirm was subject to some limitation. His approach was adopted in the following case.

Key Principle: **Where a person has no legitimate interest, financial or otherwise, in performing the contract rather than claiming damages, he ought not to be allowed to affirm it.**

Clea Shipping Corporation v. Bulk Oil International Ltd 1984

P shipowners chartered a ship to D for 24 months. The hire charge was paid in advance. After nearly a year there was a major engine failure and D refused to continue with the charter. Nevertheless P repaired the ship at a cost of £800,000. Nine months of the charter were then left. D refused to use the ship, but P did not accept their repudiation and held the ship ready to sail with a full crew until the charter expired. P claimed that they were entitled to keep the hire charge paid for the last nine months. D claimed P were only entitled to damages.

Held: (QBD) D's argument prevailed. P could not recover the hire charge because they had no legitimate interest in doing so. [1984] 1 All E.R. 129

Commentary

In *Alfred McAlpine Construction Ltd v. Panatown Ltd* 2001, HL Lord Goff stressed the importance of protecting the interest of the innocent party in having the contract performed (see pp. 46–48).

Anticipatory Breach

Key Principle: **Where there is an anticipatory breach the injured party can accept the breach and immediately claim damages.**

Hochster v. De La Tour 1853

In April 1852 D employed P to work for him as a courier in Europe from June 1. On May 11 D terminated the arrangement.

On May 22 P brought his action against D who claimed that there was no breach until June 1.

Held: P had the right to have the contract kept open until June 1. D was in breach of P's right on May 22. P could claim damages immediately. [1843–1860] All E.R. Rep. 12

Commentary
Alternatively P could have kept the contract alive until June 1 and then claimed damages.

Key Principle: **An injured party may accept a repudiatory breach simply by failing to perform their own contractual obligations.**

Vitol SA v. Norelf Ltd 1996
P agreed to purchase a cargo of propane from D. The propane was to be loaded on a ship between March 1 and 7, 1991. On March 8, P sent D a telex repudiating the contract because loading was not going to be completed until March 9. The telex was treated as an anticipatory breach. D completed the loading, informed P that it had done so, the ship sailed away, and D sold the propane to a third party but for less than half the contract price. D claimed the difference between the two prices.

Held: (HL) D, by neither affirming nor performing the contract, accepted P's repudiatory breach and were, therefore, entitled to recover damages from P. [1996] 3 W.L.R. 105

Commentary
Lord Steyn stated that whether failure to perform amounted to acceptance of a repudiatory breach depended on the particular circumstances of each case.

Key Principle: **If the injured party does not accept the anticipatory breach then damages will be assessed at the date due for performance.**

Avery v. Bowden 1856
D chartered P's ship to carry a cargo from Odessa. The ship berthed at Odessa, but D told the ship's captain that no cargo was available and that the ship should depart. The ship remained in Odessa because the captain hoped that a cargo would be found. The Crimean War broke out before the date due for performance and frustrated the contract.

Held: P's action for damages failed. (1856) 5 W.R. 45

Commentary
If the captain had accepted the breach then damages would have been recoverable.

Key Principle: **An injured party who does not accept an anticipatory breach must continue to perform their own obligations.**

Fercometal SARL v. Mediterranean Shipping Co. SA, The Simona 1988
D, shipowners, chartered a ship to P, who subsequently cancelled the charterparty. The cancellation was an anticipatory breach, which was not accepted by D. However, D failed to ensure that the vessel was ready to load on the date agreed in the charterparty, and P then cancelled on this basis.

Held: (HL) P were entitled to treat the charterparty as repudiated by D's breach and claim damages. [1988] 3 W.L.R. 200

Commentary
The injured party will only be treated as affirming the contract where they have made a clear and unequivocal decision which has been communicated to the other party.

15. REMEDIES FOR BREACH OF CONTRACT

Damages

Types of Damages Recoverable

Key Principle: The aim of damages in contract is to put the parties in as good a position as they would have been in if the contract had been performed.

Robinson v. Harman 1848
D agreed to grant P a lease of a house at a rent of £110 a year. The premises were worth considerably more. D did not have title to the house. P sued D for breach of contract.

Held: P could recover damages for the loss of his bargain as well as for his expenses. [1843–1860] All E.R. Rep. 383

Commentary
This principle is a key characteristic of a contract claim, and should be contrasted with the aim of damages in tort. It enables P to recover damages for loss of profit, and for loss of a bargain. It protects the expectation interest.

Key Principle: The aim of damages in contract is to compensate the injured party for the loss they suffered not for any gain made by the party in breach.

Surrey County Council v. Bredero Homes Ltd 1993
P sold land to D for housing development. D agreed to build in accordance with planning permission granted by the local planning authority. This allowed for the building of 72 houses. After the building work had started D obtained planning permission to build an additional five houses. P argued that D evaded the purpose of the planning permission term by failing to obtain P's agreement to the increased number of houses. D would have paid P for their agreement and P claimed damages for that loss. D accepted that in building 77 houses they were in breach of contract, and that they had increased their profit.

Held: (CA) P had suffered no loss as a result as a result of D building five more houses, and were only entitled to nominal damages. [1993] 3 All E.R. 705

Commentary
(1) The contract could have expressly provided that D pay P for each extra house built. P would then have been able to recover compensation on the above facts.
(2) In other areas of law, *e.g.* tort of trespass, it is possible for a P to recover damages in respect of D's gain.
(3) P's argument was partly based on restitution, *i.e.* unjust enrichment of D (see Chapter 1 and below).

Key Principle: **An injured party can claim damages for reliance loss instead of expectation loss in certain circumstances.**

Anglia TV v. Reed 1972
D, an actor, entered into a contract with P to play the leading role in a television play. At the last moment D withdrew and P could not find a substitute, so P abandoned the play.

Held: (CA) P were entitled to recover the expenditure they had incurred in mounting the production, both before and after they entered into the contract with D. [1972] 1 Q.B. 60

Commentary
Presumably it was easier for P to calculate their wasted expenditure than their loss of profit. Normally a plaintiff can choose whether to claim reliance loss or expectation loss.

Key Principle: **An injured party can claim restitutionary damages where there is a total failure of consideration.**

D.O. Ferguson & Associates v. Sohl 1992
P, a building contractor, entered into a contract with D for building work. The contract price was £32,194. P completed part of the work, and D had paid P £26,738, but the value of the work done was £22,065. D had the work completed by another builder for less money than the contract price. P sued D for damages and D counterclaimed for the overpayment of £4,673.

Held: (CA) D could recover the overpayment. The work had never been done by P. There was a total failure of consideration for that part of the contract. *The Times*, December 24, 1992

Key Principle: **As a general rule damages are not recoverable for injury to feelings, mental distress or damage to reputation caused by the breach of contract.**

Addis v. Gramophone Co. Ltd 1909
P was employed by D as a manager. He received a salary and earned commission. He was given six months' notice in accordance with his contract but was immediately replaced and was unable to work out his notice as manager. P was awarded damages. D appealed against that part of the award which was to compensate P for the harsh and humiliating way in which he had been dismissed.

Held: (HL) P could not recover damages for such loss. The court is not concerned with the motive or the conduct of D. Damages in contract are compensatory, not punitive or exemplary. [1909] A.C. 488

Commentary
(1) In Malik v. BCCI (in liquidation) (1997) 3 W.L.R. 95, HL distinguished Addis. In principle an employee may be able to recover damages for financial loss, arising out of loss of reputation, caused by the employer's breach of the implied duty of mutual trust and confidence in contracts of employment.
(2) In *Johnson v. Unisys 2001 Ltd* [2001] 2 W.L.R. 1076 (HL) an employee claimed damages for psychiatric injury. The majority of their Lordships considered that the implied duty of trust and confidence did not require the power of dismissal to be exercised fairly and in good faith.

Key Principle: **Where the purpose of the contract is to provide entertainment and enjoyment, damages are recoverable for disappointment, distress, upset and frustration caused by the breach.**

Jarvis v. Swan's Tours 1972
P booked a two-week "houseparty" holiday with D in a hotel in Switzerland. The brochure stated that visitors would have "a

great time". During the first week there were only 13 other guests, but there were none during the second week, and the hotel proprietor did not speak English.

Held: (CA) P was entitled to be compensated for his loss of enjoyment. [1973] 1 Q.B. 233

Commentary
See also *Jackson v. Horizon Holidays* (1975) (see p. 44). Damages are not normally recoverable for anguish and vexation caused by breach of an ordinary commercial contract.

Key Principle: **Where the purpose of the contract is to provide relief from mental distress, damages are recoverable.**

Heywood v. Wellers 1976
P employed D solicitors to obtain and enforce an injunction to prevent a man molesting her. The solicitors were negligent, and as a result she was molested on three or four occasions.

Held: (CA) P was entitled to damages for mental distress. [1976] Q.B. 446

Key principle: **Where a major or important object of the contract is to give pleasure, relaxation or peace of mind, damages are recoverable for loss of amenity.**

Farley v. Skinner 2001
P was considering buying a country house about 15 miles from Gatwick International Airport. He wanted to be reasonably sure that the property was not seriously affected by aircraft noise, and asked D, a surveyor, to inspect the house and in particular to investigate whether the property would be affected by aircraft noise. He told the surveyor that he did not want a property on a flight path. The surveyor stated that it was unlikely that the property suffered greatly from aircraft noise. In fact the house was close to a navigation beacon and was markedly affected by aircraft noise. P sought damages from D because his use and enjoyment of the property was impaired by the aircraft noise.

Held: (HL) D was in breach of his contractual obligation to provide P with accurate information about the aircraft noise. D was entitled to damages for being deprived of the chance of making an informed choice whether or not to buy the property which resulted in mental distress and disappointment. The award of £10,000 by the judge for loss of amenity was confirmed, although it was considered by their Lordships to be on the high side. [2001] 3 W.L.R. 899

Commentary
(1) Their Lordships applied *Ruxley Electronics v. Forsyth* (see below) in holding held that P was entitled to damages for loss of amenity (an example of non-pecuniary damages).
(2) Their Lordships considered that P could alternatively have recovered damages under the principle in *Watts v. Morrow* (see below).

Key Principle: **Where the mental distress is caused by the physical consequences of the breach, damages are recoverable.**

Watts v. Morrow 1991
D, a building surveyor, negligently surveyed a house for P, who had indicated to D that they wanted to buy a trouble-free holiday home. P purchased the house for £177,500. P soon discovered that major internal and external repairs needed to be undertaken promptly. The repairs took approximately six months to complete.

Held: (CA) P was entitled to a modest sum of £750 as compensation for the discomfort suffered from having to live in a house undergoing major repairs. [1991] 1 W.L.R. 1421

Commentary
(1) In *Farley v. Skinner* (above) Lord Scott considered that "physical" in the context of physical inconvenience and discomfort means "sensory (sight, touch, hearing, smell, etc.) experience".
(2) See also p. 169 on measure of damages.

Causation

Key Principle: **The breach of contract must be the effective cause of the injured party's loss.**

Cossey v. Lonnkvist 2000

D agreed to buy a butcher's shop from P. An accountant X agreed to assist D obtain finance from a bank for the purchase. The bank asked X for details of the trading activity for the year up to the end of June 1991. X provided details, but relied on out of date information that covered the period up to December 1990, and did not check the 1991 figures. D obtained the finance and purchased the shop, but it ran at a loss. P sued D for the balance of the purchase price. Part of D's defence was that X owed them a duty of care in the preparation projections of the shop's likely profitability.

Held: (CA) X was in breach of the contractual duty owed to D to exercise due care in providing accurate information to the bank. D suffered loss because they purchased a business which subsequently failed, which they might not have purchased had they known of downturn in trading in 1991. X did not owe D a duty to alert them to such a downturn. Therefore, D's breach did not cause D's loss. [2000] Lloyd's Rep. PN 885

Commentary

(1) Sir Anthony Evans (dissenting) held that the chain of causation was not broken because X's breach deprived D of the opportunity for reconsideration and not proceeding to buy the shop.
(2) Compare *Stovold v. Barlows* (1995) (see p. 174).

Remoteness of Damage

Key Principle: **Damages are recoverable for loss or damage which arise naturally from the breach in the ordinary course of things, or which were in the contemplation of the parties at the time they entered into the contract.**

Hadley v. Baxendale 1854

P's mill in Gloucester was brought to a standstill by a broken crankshaft. P engaged D a carrier to take the crankshaft to London where it was to be used as a pattern for a new one. D, in breach of contract, delayed delivery by five days. Unknown to D, P only had one crankshaft and so the mill was out of action for longer than need be. P claimed damages for loss of profit caused by this delay.

Held: P could not recover such loss, because it could not fairly and reasonably be considered to arise naturally from the breach. [1843–1860] All E.R. Rep. 461

Commentary
(1) If P had told D at the time of entering the contract that this was the mill's only crankshaft, P could have recovered under the second limb of the principle.
(2) Although this principle has been refined in later cases, it remains an accurate statement of the law.

Key Principle: **The test of remoteness is whether the loss is reasonably foreseeable as liable to result from the breach, bearing in mind the knowledge, imputed or actual, of the party in breach.**

Victoria Laundry (Windsor) Ltd v. Newman Industries Ltd 1949
D sold a large boiler to P who were launderers and dyers. D knew that P wanted the boiler for immediate use in their business. The boiler was delivered five months late. P sued D for the loss of profits during that period.

Held: (CA) P could recover for loss of profits on the ordinary laundry business. They could not recover damages for the loss of profits that they would have made on lucrative dyeing contracts, because D did not know of these contracts at the time they entered into the contract with P. [1949] 1 All E.R. 997

Commentary
(1) Imputed and actual knowledge correspond to the two limbs of the principle in *Hadley v. Baxendale* (1854) (see p. 166).
(2) Asquith L.J. used the phrase "reasonable foreseeability" as opposed to "reasonable contemplation".

Key Principle: **The question is whether a reasonable man in D's position would realise that P's loss was sufficiently likely to result from the breach.**

Koufos v. C. Czarnikow Ltd, The Heron II 1967

P chartered D's ship to carry a cargo of sugar to Basrah. In breach of the charterparty the ship deviated from its route which delayed its arrival by nine days. The market price of sugar had fallen during that period.

Held: (HL) P could recover the difference between the price for which the sugar was sold and the price at which it would have been sold if there had been no delay. [1967] 3 W.L.R. 1491

Commentary

The phrase "reasonable foreseeability" does not mean the same as "reasonable foreseeability" in the test for remoteness in the tort of negligence. In contract there should be a serious possibility that the particular consequences would occur whereas in tort it would be enough if there was a slight possibility.

Key Principle: **The test of remoteness should result in the same amount of damages being recoverable whether a plaintiff brings an action in contract or in tort.**

Parsons (Livestock) Ltd v. Uttley Ingham & Co. Ltd 1977

D supplied and installed a bulk food storage hopper for P, who were pig farmers. D forgot to unseal the ventilator and the pignuts stored in the hopper went mouldy. As a result of being fed the nuts 254 pigs died. P claimed damages for breach of contract, including a claim for loss of sales and turnover. D claimed that damages for loss of sales and turnover were too remote.

Held: (CA) D were liable for the loss of the pigs that died, but not for loss of profit on future sales. [1977] 3 W.L.R. 990

Commentary

(1) Lord Denning considered that the test of remoteness should depend not upon whether the claim was brought in contract or in

tort, but upon whether the claim was for physical damage or for loss of profit.

(2) Lord Scarman suggested that there is no substantive difference between reasonable foreseeability in tort and reasonable contemplation in contract.

Key Principle: **Where services are supplied to a party for an activity which involves complicated construction or manufacturing techniques the supplier should not be expected to have in their reasonable contemplation details of these techniques.**

Balfour Beatty Construction (Scotland) Ltd v. Scottish Power plc 1994
P were building a bypass, which involved constructing a concrete aqueduct over the road. D agreed to provide P with a temporary supply of electricity to a concrete batching plant. An electricity supply failure caused the plant to cease operating. Unknown to D the construction of the aqueduct required a continuous pour of concrete. As a result of the supply failure, not only could the aqueduct not be completed, it had to be demolished and rebuilt.

Held: (HL) P could not recover damages to cover the cost of demolishing and rebuilding the aqueduct. *The Times,* March 23, 1994

Measure of Damages

Key Principle: **In a contract for the sale of goods damages are normally assessed using the difference in value between the market price and the contract price.**

Wertheim v. Chicoutimi Pulp Co. 1911
P agreed to buy wood pulp from D. It was delivered seven months late by which time the market price had fallen from £3.50 per ton to £2.12 per ton. P's loss was £1.38 per ton. However, P had resold the wood pulp at £3.00 per ton.

Held: (JCPC) Because of the resale D was only liable to pay damages to P of 50p per ton. [1911] A.C. 301

Commentary

(1) This principle is to be found is section 50(3) (remedy for the seller) and section 51(3) (remedy for the buyer) of the Sale of Goods Act 1979. Where the goods sold have a latent defect the buyer may recover the actual loss suffered rather than the difference in value: *Bence Graphics International Ltd v. Fasson U.K. Ltd* [1997] 1 All E.R. 979.

(2) The difference in value test is used in the majority of contract cases where there is a claim for expectation loss.

Key Principle: **Where there is no available market the seller can still recover damages for loss of profit.**

WL Thompson Ltd v. R. Robinson (Gunmakers) Ltd 1955

D refused to accept delivery of a new car from P, car dealers. There was no demand for the car, so P mitigated their loss by persuading the manufacturers to take back the car.

Held: (Ch D) P were entitled to recover damages for the lost profit. [1955] 2 W.L.R. 185

Commentary

If P could have sold the car to another customer at the same or a higher price then P would only be able to recover nominal damages: *Charter v. Sullivan* [1957] 2 W.L.R. 528.

Key Principle: **If a party to a contract fails to provide the standard of service agreed the other party can claim damages for the difference in value between the standard agreed and that received.**

White Arrow Express Ltd v. Lamey's Distribution Ltd 1995

P operated a mail order business and entered into a contract with D, who agreed to deliver and collect goods sold to customers. P claimed damages for D's failure to provide the enhanced level of service for which they had paid.

Held: (CA) P had not submitted specific evidence of the difference in value between what they contracted for and what they received. Therefore, they were only entitled to nominal damages. *The Times*, July 21, 1995

Commentary
The difficulty P faced was in quantifying what damage/loss they had suffered as a result of the breach. The Court of Appeal considered that if A hired and paid in advance for a four-door saloon at £200 a day and received delivery of a two-door saloon available for £100 a day, he suffered loss; the measure of damages being the difference between the price paid and the market value of what was obtained.

Key Principle: **In building work the cost of reinstatement is the normal measure of damages.**

East Ham Corporation v. Bernard Sunley & Sons Ltd 1966
D, a building contractor, defectively attached cast stone panels to the external walls of a school owned by P. The panels fell off.

Held: (HL) P could recover as damages the cost of reinstating the panels, rather than the difference or diminution in value of the property. It was reasonable for P to insist upon reinstatement. [1966] A.C. 406

Commentary
This test for measure of damages is often described at the "cost of cure".

Key Principle: **The cost of reinstatement can be recovered so long as it represents the loss suffered.**

Tito v. Waddell (No. 2) 1977
In 1913 an agreement was made with the landowners of Ocean Island to mine for phosphate. It was a term of the agreement that the mining company would return all the worked out land to the owners and would replant the land with food-bearing trees. Most of the island had been mined and islanders no longer lived on the island. P, an islander, brought an action for damages against D because no replanting had occurred. Should

the measure of damages be the cost of replanting or the difference in value between the replanted island and the island as it was?

Held: (Ch D) P was entitled to damages for the difference in value. It was unreasonable to treat as a loss the cost of replanting which was unlikely to be done. P owned small scattered plots of land, other islanders might not replant, and P was now settled elsewhere on a larger island unaffected by mining. [1977] 2 W.L.R. 496

Key Principle: **In deciding whether to award the cost of reinstatement the court should take into account whether P intends to reinstate and whether that intention is reasonable.**

Radford v. De Froberville 1977

P sold part of his land to D who agreed to build a brick boundary wall on her land. D failed to do so and sold her property. P sued D for the cost of building such a wall on his side of the boundary.

Held: (Ch D) P could recover the cost because he intended to build the wall and it was reasonable for him to do so. [1977] 1 W.L.R. 1262

Commentary

In *Ruxley Electronics Ltd v. Forsyth* (1995) (see p. 173) the House of Lords placed more emphasis on the requirement of reasonableness. P's intention should only be relevant in so far as it affects reasonableness.

Key Principle: **The diminution in value rule is almost always appropriate where property is acquired following negligent advice by surveyors.**

Watts v. Morrow 1991

P instructed D, a building surveyor, to survey a house. D negligently carried out the survey. P then purchased the house for £177,500. P discovered that major internal and external repairs were needed. P claimed £33,961 as damages, being the cost of the repairs.

Held: (CA) P was entitled to damages of £15,000 being the difference between the value of the property as represented by D and its true value. [1991] 1 W.L.R. 1421

Commentary

P is compensated for the loss caused by D's negligent breach of contract, *e.g.* paying more for a house than it was worth. D did not promise that no repairs other than those noted in the survey, were needed. See also *Banque Bruxelles Lambert SA v. Eagle Star Insurance Co Ltd* [1996] 3 W.L.R. 87, HL in respect of negligent valuations for commercial purchasers.

Key Principle: **Where the cost of reinstatement is out of proportion to the benefit obtained by P then damages should be assessed by reference to the diminution in value of the property.**

Ruxley Electronics and Constructions Ltd v. Forsyth 1995

P sued D for the balance due on a contract to build a swimming pool in D's garden. D claimed that P were in breach of contract by building the pool six feet deep when it was agreed that the pool should be built to a depth of seven feet six inches deep. The county court judge found as a matter of fact that the shallower pool did not affect the value of D's property. D counter-claimed damages of £21,560 being the cost of rebuilding the pool to the correct depth.

Held: (HL) P could not recover damages for the cost of reinstatement. Their Lordships agreed that there was no diminution in the value of P's property but awarded P £2,500 for loss of amenity. [1995] 3 W.L.R. 118.

Commentary

(1) Their Lordships placed considerable emphasis on the requirement that it should be reasonable to incur the cost of reinstatement. On the facts of this case it was unreasonable to incur the cost of demolishing the existing pool and building a newer and deeper one.

(2) See also *Farley v. Skinner* (above) on damages for loss of amenity.

Damages for Loss of a Chance

Key Principle: **The loss of a right to belong to a limited class of competitors is of pecuniary value for which damages can be awarded.**

Chaplin v. Hicks 1911
D advertised in a national newspaper inviting applications from female readers for work in the theatre. There were 12 positions which would last three years. 10 applicants were to be short-listed in each of five areas by readers of the newspaper. D would then select 12 from the shortlist of 50. P came top of her area, but was not given a reasonable opportunity of presenting herself for the final selection by D.

Held: (CA) P was awarded damages because she lost the advantage of being in the final selection. [1911] 2 K.B. 786

Key Principle: **The court should evaluate the loss of P's chance rather than consider on a balance of probabilities whether the breach caused P's loss.**

Stovold v. Barlows 1995
P received an offer of £505,000 for his house from X. D solicitors were instructed to carry out the necessary legal formalities. Five days after D agreed to send the title deeds and a draft contract, X's solicitors had still not received them. X then decided to purchase another property. P's house was subsequently sold at a lower price and P claimed damages of £96,312.

Held: (CA) The chance of the purchase going ahead was 50 per cent and so the plaintiff was entitled to 50 per cent of the damages claimed. *The Times*, October 30, 1995

Commentary
The judge at first instance considered that there was an issue of causation. P had shown on a balance of probabilities that if the

documents had arrived on time then X would have bought P's property. Therefore P could recover his full loss. CA disagreed with the judge's approach and considered that even if the documents had arrived on time X might still have decided to buy the other house.

Mitigation

Key Principle: **The injured party is under a duty to take all reasonable steps to mitigate any loss consequent on the breach.**

British Westinghouse Electric and Manufacturing Co. v. Underground Electric Railways Co. of London Ltd 1912
P agreed to supply D with turbines, but the turbines supplied did not meet the contract specification. D used the turbines for several years, but then replaced them. The replacement turbines were more efficient. P claimed the unpaid balance of the contract price. D counterclaimed and recovered the increased cost of operating D's machines, but also claimed the cost of replacing them.

Held: (HL) D could not recover the cost of the new turbines. D was not under a duty to mitigate by buying new turbines. The cost of operating them was less than the cost of operating D's turbines. Those savings had to be set off against the cost of buying them. [1911–1913] All E.R. Rep. 63

Commentary
If the injured party does not take reasonable steps to mitigate their loss then they are not able to obtain damages for that loss.

Key Principle: **In commercial contracts the duty to mitigate will often require the injured party to enter into a new contract with the contract-breaker.**

Payzu v. Saunders 1919
D agreed to sell goods to P over a period of nine months. Payment was to be made within one month of delivery. P failed to pay the first instalment in time. D refused to continue to

deliver on these terms, but offered to continue to supply P if P agreed to pay cash with each order. P refused and as a result sustained considerable losses.

Held: (CA) P should have accepted D's offer. As a result of not doing so they sustained a large measure of loss which they ought to have avoided. [1918–1919] All E.R. Rep. 219

Key Principle: **The injured party has to give credit for benefits arising directly from the consequences of the breach.**

Hussey v. Eels 1990
P purchased a bungalow from D for £53,250 in reliance on a misrepresentation that the property had not been subject to subsidence. The true value of the bungalow was £36,250. P could not afford to stabilise the foundations. After two years of living in the house P applied for and eventually obtained planning permission to demolish their bungalow and build two new bungalows on the land. P then sold the land with planning permission for £78,500. The county court judge rejected P's claim for £17,000 on the ground that their gain on the re-sale wiped out their initial loss.

Held: (CA) P were entitled to damages of £17,000. The profit on the resale was not a direct consequence of D's breach. P bought the house to live in, not for its development potential. [1990] 2 Q.B. 227

Commentary
This principle was also applied in the *British Westinghouse* case (see p. 175).

Contributory Negligence

Key Principle: **Where D is in breach of a contractual duty of care and a duty of care in tort, the defence of contributory negligence is available to D.**

Forsikringsaktieselskapet Vesta v. Butcher 1988
P, a large Norwegian insurance company were liable under an insurance policy for damage caused to a fish farm on the coast

of Norway by a severe gale. P had reinsured with Lloyds of London. D was an insurance broker. P sued D both for breach of contract and the tort of negligence when D refused to pay under the reinsurance contract.

Held: (CA) The defence of contributory negligence was available to D, who were only 25 per cent to blame for P's loss. [1988] 3 W.L.R. 565

Commentary
(1) In QBD, Hobhouse J. identified three types of situations:

  (i) where D is in breach of a strict contractual duty;

  (ii) where D is in breach of a contractual but not a tortious duty of care; and

  (iii) as in this case.

(2) The case went to the House of Lords but not on this point.

Key Principle: **Where D is in breach of a strict contractual provision which does not depend upon a failure to take reasonable care the defence of contributory negligence is not available to D.**

Barclays Bank PLC v. Fairclough Building Ltd 1994

D agreed with P to clean and treat the asbestos roofs of two buildings used by P for the storage of documents. In breach of the contract D did not use specialist contractors and did not use workmanship that was "the best of its kind". As a result the buildings were contaminated by asbestos dust, which would cost £4 million to remove. D argued that P were at fault in failing to ensure that D fulfilled its obligations under the contract.

Held: (CA) P's claim should not be reduced. The defence of contributory negligence was not available to D. In any event, P was not under a duty to prevent D from committing breaches of the contract. [1994] 3 W.L.R. 1057

Commentary
This decision corresponds with the recommendations of the Law Commission in 1993 in its report, *Contributory Negligence as a Defence in Contract* (Report No. 219).

Penalty Clauses

Key Principle: **A penalty clause is aimed at punishing the party in breach and is invalid.**

Dunlop Pneumatic Tyre Co. Ltd v. New Garage & Motor Co Ltd 1915

P, tyre manufacturers, supplied tyres to D, who agreed not to sell the tyres to retailers at a price below the manufacturer's list price. If D did sell or offer to sell the tyres below this price then D had to pay P £5 by way of liquidated damages.

Held: (HL) The obligation to pay £5 was not a penalty clause, and so was enforceable by P. [1915] A.C. 79

Commentary
A liquidated damages clause is a genuine pre-estimate of the damage likely to be caused by the breach.

Key Principle: **In determining whether a clause was a penalty clause the court should not normally consider hypothetical situations which might result in the damages paid being substantially more than the loss suffered.**

Philips Hong Kong Ltd v. A-G of Hong Kong 1993

P agreed with the Hong Kong government to design, supply and install a computerised supervisory system for new roads and tunnels. The agreement contained clauses which provided for fixed sums of money to be paid if work was not completed by certain key dates. P sought a declaration that the clauses were unenforceable.

Held: (JCPC) P had not established that the clauses were penal. The issue had to be determined objectively judged at the time the contract was made. *The Times*, February 15, 1993

Commentary
Lord Woolf considered that what the parties had agreed should normally be upheld. Any other approach would lead to uncertainty which was undesirable, especially in commercial contracts.

Equitable Remedies

Key Principle: **Specific performance is an exceptional discretionary remedy.**

Cooperative Insurance Society Ltd v. Argyll Stores (Holdings Ltd) 1997

D leased their supermarket premises from P. The supermarket was operating at a loss. It comprised 30 per cent of the letting area of the Hillsborough Shopping Centre. D decided to sell it and on not finding a buyer had closed and stripped out the supermarket despite a "keep open" covenant. It would cost £1 million to reinstate the supermarket. P applied for an order of specific performance.

Held: (HL) Such a covenant was not normally specifically enforceable because precise formulation of the order would be difficult; and, if the order was not complied with, the punishment of contempt was heavy-handed and unsuitable. [1997] 3 All E.R. 297.

Commentary

In *Highland and Universal Properties Ltd v. Safeway Properties Ltd*, *The Times*, March 22, 2000, the Inner House of the Court of Session (Scotland) was to prepared to grant an order requiring the tenant of retail premises to keep them open for trading. The Lord President stated that Scottish experience did not bear out the House of Lord's fears.

Key Principle: **An order for specific performance may be made where damages would be nominal only.**

Beswick v. Beswick 1968

(See p. 43 for facts).

Held: (HL) P suing as administrator would only be entitled to nominal damages because her deceased husband's estate had not suffered any loss. Specific performance was granted. [1968] A.C. 58

Key Principle: **An order for specific performance is unlikely to be made where it would cause severe hardship to D.**

Patel v. Ali 1984

D sold her house to P. There was a four-year delay before P sought an order of specific performance.

Held: The order was not granted because of D's disabling illness, which made her dependent on her neighbours, and her husband's bankruptcy. Both of these events occurred after the sale. [1984] 1 All E.R. 978

Commentary

Examples of cases where an application for specific performance was refused, although not on the grounds of hardship to D are: *Gibson v. Manchester City Council* (no agreement); *Redgrave v. Hurd* (contract rescinded for misrepresentation); *Shell U.K. Ltd v. Lostock Garages Ltd* (P acted unfairly).

Key Principle: **Where the grant of an injunction would be oppressive, damages in lieu would be appropriate.**

Jaggard v. Sawyer 1995

P purchased a house in a housing development on a private road. Each house was conveyed subject to a restrictive covenant: not to use any unbuilt land other than as a garden. In 1987 D bought a house on the development. They then bought a piece of land with no right of access to the road and obtained planning permission to build a house. P objected but only applied for an injunction once the house was almost built.

Held: (CA) The injunction was not granted. [1995] 1 W.L.R. 269

Commentary

If P had applied for an interlocutory injunction before the house was built the court considered that it would have been granted.

Key Principle: **Where there is a contract for personal services the court will not generally grant an injunction where that would compel the performance of the contract.**

Page One Records v. Britton 1968

P, the manager of D (The Troggs pop group), claimed that he had been dismissed and sought an injunction to prevent them from employing another manager.

Held: (Ch D) P's application was refused because D could not work without a manager and the effect of an injunction would be to force D to continue to employ P. [1968] 1 W.L.R. 157

Commentary

(1) An order of specific performance will not be issued for the same reason.

(2) Prohibitory injunctions are often the main remedy where there is a breach of a valid contract in restraint of trade (e.g. *Bridge v. Deacons* (1984)) (see p. 134).

Limitation Periods

Key Principle: **In an action for relief from the consequences of a mistake the requirement that "reasonable diligence" be used to discover the mistake, means doing what an ordinary prudent person would do in the circumstances.**

Peco Arts Inc. v. Hazlitt Gallery Ltd 1983

P purchased a drawing from D for $18,000 relying on the recommendation of an expert. It was a term of the contract that the drawing was by Ingres. In fact it was a copy. P discovered the mistake 11 years after the purchase when it was revalued for the second time. D admitted liability to return the price paid, but argued that the claim was statute-barred.

Held: (QBD) P obtained rescission and recovery of the purchase price. P had been reasonably diligent having relied on an expert, and the reputation of D, as well as the fact that the first revaluation did not reveal that the drawing was a copy. [1983] 1 W.L.R. 1315

Commentary

(1) The Limitation Act 1980, s.32(1)(c) provides that the period of limitation runs from when P could with reasonable diligence have discovered the mistake.

(2) See common mistake (p. 98).
(3) Presumably P did not sue for breach of contract because such a claim would have been statute-barred (Limitation Act 1980, s.5: six years).
(4) *Leaf v. International Galleries* (1950) was distinguished.

Key Principle: **Equitable remedies such as rescission for misrepresentation are subject to the equitable principle that delay defeats equity.**

Leaf v. International Galleries 1950
(For facts see p. 89).

Held: (CA) P could not, five years after the purchase, choose to repudiate the contract because of D's breach. P had accepted the picture. If P claimed rescission for misrepresentation that too was defeated by P's delay.

INDEX